The

Good Life

in

Galicia

2019

Cyberworld Publishing

www.cyberworldpublishing.com

This book is copyright © S Bush 2019
First published by Cyberworld Publishing in 2019
Cover design: Copyright Cyberworld Publishing 2019

Cover photo: Road in Ribeiras de Miño, in the Ribeira
Sacra region of Galicia: Copyright: Pacoma 2019

E-book ISBN: 978-1-922187-50-5
Print ISBN: 978-0-9953961-9-7

The Good life in Galicia 2019

An Anthology of Prose and Poetry

Compiled from *The Good Life in Galicia 2019*
competition entries and invited works.

S. Bush Ed.

Table of Contents

Introduction

Now in its fourth year, this anthology, *The Good Life in Galicia 2019*, and the Good Life in Galicia competition behind it, began in 2016 as an idea for a competition to encourage people to write about Galicia and raise awareness internationally of this fascinating part of Green Spain. As we are an English-language publisher, the stories had to be in English, and to make it easy, entrants did not have to have lived in Galicia or even to have visited here. These requirements remained the same for the 2018 ans 2019 editions and will continue to apply to the 2020 competition, but in 2017 we added a poetry category, as Galicia, one of the Celtic lands, is a land of poets. Hence again this year there is a plethora of good poetry here.

We were pleased in 2019 to have had entries in all categories from Galicians.

There were outstanding contest entries in each category, and our judges had a difficult time choosing their winners. Winner in the fiction and non-fiction categories was Dawn Hawkins, with "Jo's Journey" and "The Chimney Fire" respectively, both very different stories.

In poetry, the winner was also Dawn Hawkins with her evocative poem "Galician Mist".

The bulk of this anthology comprises competition entries with the addition of works submitted for inclusion by several local and international authors.

We hope you enjoy this fourth, brief look at an ancient land, one full of generous people and natural splendours, and agree that there is indeed a lot of good in a life in Galicia.

~

Rose in Ruins

Liza Grantham

In Pontevedra, Pete and Rose had bought an old stone ruin,
They couldn't move in straight away—it needed so much doin'.
They'd stay here for the summer months and take a long vacation,
Then come again in early spring to start the renovation.
The end of summer came too fast, Rose said to Pete: "Let's stay!
We'll rent a small apartment and . . . ." "Forget it, Rose, no way!"
But Rose was quite impulsive and so keen to relocate
Despite poor Pete's insistence she decided not to wait.
She bought a little camping stove, a sleeping bag, a tent,
"I wish you'd change your mind," she sighed, but Pete would not relent.
So, Pete went back to England, leaving Rose to do her thing
"She'll give up soon enough," he thought, "she'll never last 'til spring!"

Rose made new friends who asked about her living situation:
"You've water and electrics, Rose? You've started restoration?"
She'd look at them and, laughing, said "Electrics? Water? Pardon?
It doesn't even have a roof; I'm camping in the garden!
I'd ask you round to dinner but I have nowhere to cook it
I'm eating mainly bread and cheese, I'm peeing in a bucket!"
"You can't camp out when autumn comes, the days and nights grow colder,
You'll need a little heated room—we'll work on it," they told her.
They chose the tiny outhouse, it would need a roof and floor,
But, with a wood stove burning, it would soon warm up for sure.
As soon as they began the roof, they knew they were in trouble
The slightest banging on the beams reduced the walls to rubble!

The autumn nights brought bitter cold, the new room still not finished,
And hopes for its completion now had totally diminished.

No way would Rose admit defeat, not in a month of Sundays!
She bought a thicker sleeping bag and proper thermal undies!
Then came the storms, fierce winds and hail, the tent was torn and tattered,
Rose stood her ground, would not lose face, although her nerves were shattered.
The weather worsened week by week, much colder, darker, wetter,
She bought a leaky caravan; it wasn't that much better!
At last poor Rose could stand no more—so much for sunny Spain!
She drove down to the wifi bar and booked a homeward plane.
Then Pete rang up "I've changed my mind! Guess what? I'm coming over!"
"No *don't!*" she wailed, "Too late!" he laughed, "My ferry's just left Dover!"

Mi Suegra's Kitchen

Michele Northwood

(Third place Prose Fiction 2019)

September 2019

I could not believe it. It had taken me twenty years, but I was finally cooking in my mother-in-law's kitchen! For the first time ever, I was alone in the house, standing in the inner sanctum of her domain, completely in charge of producing a meal fit for my four *cuñados* (brother-in-laws), a handful of nieces and nephews, and of course, the lady herself, my *suegra*, Pilar.

Unlike in my own home in Murcia, where I would tend to put things on the stove, wander off, do other things and usually be reminded that I was supposed to be cooking when the distinct smell of burning molested my nostrils, this time I was leaving nothing to chance.

Pilar had been called away on a matter of great importance—something that I had not been privy to. She had barked orders at a rapid pace, pointing to an oven full of roasting meat, a hob full of bubbling pans, a sizzling frying pan, and an abundance of bowls and plates of other foodstuffs that all needed special attention and different cooking times. I stood guard vigilantly as though my life depended on it.

As I stirred a pan of green beans and corn, both grown from the *huerta* (orchard/vegetable patch) in the back garden and tried in vain to remember all her hastily delivered instructions, I was taken back more than twenty years to when I was about to visit my husband's (then boyfriend's) family for the first time.

It was September 1997, and my pulse was racing as Daniel slowed the car to a steady halt in front of a large stone house. It was surrounded by a huge plot of land and a forest of imposing pine trees that towered majestically over the home in an almost protective manner, casting shade on the surrounding land.

"We're here," he said, meaning that after travelling from the south of Spain for two days, we had finally arrived at his parents' house.

In the time it took me to reach down into the foot-well and extricate my bag, Daniel was out of the car and staring at me through the passenger door window.

"You stay there. I´ll only be a few minutes," he said and strode towards the front door.

I sat back in my seat, stunned. What did he mean, "you stay there"? Why was I not being introduced to the family? Was I an embarrassment to him because I was a *guiri*, a foreigner, who had no right to be dating a Galician?

Daniel's few minutes turned into twenty, and my anger and exasperation were coming to the boil by the time he reappeared.

"Okay, let's go," he said, starting the engine and pulling out into the traffic.

I concentrated on keeping my lips firmly closed. Although I was hurt and angry, I did not want to start a major argument when we had only been in Meaño for less than half an hour. Minutes later, Daniel slowed the car again and drove onto the driveway of another huge, three-story dwelling just down the street from his parents' house. He jumped out, but I remained seated. Was I supposed to stay in the car again? Who was he visiting this time, another family member?

"Come on!" Daniel said impatiently, staring at me with consternation through the passenger window. "This is where we're staying."

A distant relative, who would conveniently be out of town, had offered us her home for our visit. We would have the entire place to ourselves. I stepped out of the car into typical Galician September weather—cold, drizzly and overcast—which also conveniently described the house's interior. It was so overwhelming damp and freezing cold from lack of use that we virtually lived in one room, the bedroom, only venturing to the kitchen or bathroom when needs must.

For the first couple of days, I began to feel like an escaped prisoner evading capture as my partner wandered off to spend time with his parents whilst I stayed encapsulated within the confines of the dreary, cold house. Feeling disillusioned, I could usually be found sitting as close as was humanly possible to an electric radiator, a source of heat that also seemed to be suffering from severe depression, as it showed very little enthusiasm and had literally no intention of doing its job.

On the third day, when Daniel returned to find me hugging the heater, he stared at me in dismay as though I had seriously lost the plot.

"Get ready, we're all going out for lunch," he said, shaking his head despondently. I had yet to establish who "we all" referred to, but I diligently set about getting dressed, feeling slightly more enthusiastic about escaping the confines of the house for a while and meeting other people.

We set off walking uphill and one hundred metres up the road another couple sprang out and walked in step beside us. They nodded and grunted to Daniel, who reciprocated their greeting. They glanced fleetingly in my direction and looked away. I was there, but unimportant. As no introductions were forthcoming, and I felt too uncomfortable to introduce myself, I wandered on in silence.

Another hundred metres further up the hill the trip came to an abrupt stop. Panicking muttering and fidgeting took place. Their nervousness spread to me like an infection. I got the jitters without really understanding why.

"What's going on?" I eventually asked, feeling like a complete outsider.

"This is my mum and dad's house," Daniel explained.

"Yeah . . . and?"

"Well, because we are five brothers, my mum always told us that we couldn't bring girlfriends home."

"Oh, I see," I replied, realising that was probably the reason why I had been left sitting in the car and then the house for the past three days.

"She said it would get really confusing, you know, having loads of different girls wandering around, so we could only bring a girl home if the relationship was serious."

"Oh, okay," I said, wondering if a marriage proposal might be in the making! "So, who are these?" I pointed absently at the other couple and grinned. "Moral support?"

"Err, this is my brother, Javier, and his girlfriend, Lydia," Daniel explained.

"*Hola!*" I said, smiling as they finally made firm eye contact and we did the obligatory kissing of both cheeks.

"Javier has been seeing Lydia for the past twelve years," Daniel continued, "But this is the first time he has brought her to the house."

"WHAT?" I exclaimed, seriously wondering what type of dragon I was about to meet if his brother had taken more than a decade to bring his girlfriend home!

"Yeah, so, we decided to introduce you both at the same time."

My mind was whirling uncontrollably. Did they need moral support to face their mother? Now I was scared!

Javier pushed his girlfriend further towards the front door.

"Ring the bell," he ordered.

I was positioned slightly behind her and the brothers stood at the rear. I could not help but feel like cannon fodder as I awaited my fate.

Being coaxed by Javier, Lydia lifted her hand towards the bell, pressed it, and then totally freaked out.

"I can´t do it!" she said, running to stand behind him.

As the door slowly opened, I was on the front line and in firing range.

"*Mamá, esta is Michele,*" Daniel said, from somewhere in the background. His mother eyed me suspiciously and formally shook my hand.

"*Esta es Lydia, Mamá,*" Javier added, as his girlfriend slinked to the front and held out her hand.

I was immediately shocked when Pilar opened her arms and embraced Lydia like a long-lost daughter. What a difference! I felt so belittled and close to tears. Was she demonstrating her preference for a Spanish daughter-in-law? Had she taken an instant dislike to me? Didn't she want her son dating a foreigner?

"Don't worry," I heard Daniel whisper. "My mum knows her mum."

I stood there feeling uncomfortable, clueless as to any future plans and only understanding a quarter of what was being said as I listened to the familiar Galician twang, their lilting accents rising and falling with ease.

As everyone headed for the door and I surmised that we were leaving, Pilar flipped open her coat like a flasher in a park to reveal a black cardigan with fur trim.

"*Mira!*" she said, smiling at Daniel. "This is the cardigan you sent me."

"Great," said my partner.

"Oh, poo!" I thought. I was wearing the exact same attire under my coat!

"Come on," Daniel said, taking my arm as everyone continued to move towards the front door. "We're all going to a restaurant."

"No, we're not," I whispered harshly. "Take me back to the house. I've got to change!"

"Whatever for?"

"There is no way I want to be seen wearing the same attire as your mother!" I replied.

* * * *

The following day, wearing my pyjamas, dressing gown, and a big, thick coat, I ventured downstairs into the freezing-cold kitchen to try to make some breakfast. In the only pan I could find, I set about boiling water for coffee and in the absence of any other receptacles, I slapped a piece of sliced bread directly onto the electric hob in a vain attempt at making toast. As usual, my mind was wandering, and as I perused the kitchen for a few minutes, examining strange utensils and other unfamiliar paraphernalia, the doorbell rang. Daniel was still in the land of nod, so I ventured to the front door.

"*Buenos días.*" My future mother-in-law eyed my weird attire, smiled thinly, and invited herself inside.

"*Hola,*" I said as I shuffled after her into the kitchen. As soon as we entered, the familiar smell of burnt toast hit my nostrils and I cringed as Pilar looked from the stove to me with a look of sheer exasperation.

"Let's open the window, shall we?" she said, whilst simultaneously turning off the stove, picking up the burnt effigy that no longer resembled bread, and throwing it out of the window.

"I couldn´t find a toaster," I weakly explained.

Pilar´s facial expression made me wither under her gaze. I felt like I was six years old and had been caught playing with a box of matches.

"*Dondé está mi hijo?*"

"Your son is still in bed," I replied, wondering if she intended to rescue him before I succeeded in burning the house down. Picking up a dishcloth, I began to scrub the electric hob as though my life depended on it. Pilar stared disdainfully in my direction and then took advantage of my distraction by turning on her heels and marching up the stairs.

Intrigued, I drifted to the bottom of the staircase with the dishcloth still in my hand and honed my ears, trying unsuccessfully to hear the mother/son conversation. A muttered exchange lasting less than two minutes was followed by Daniel exiting the bedroom fully dressed and bouncing down the stairs, his mother close behind him as I made a hasty retreat back to the kitchen.

I busied myself with the hot water and coffee cups in a vain attempt to look efficient when my future mother-in-law walked in, but Daniel entered alone. Seconds later, I heard the front door close.

"Where's your mum?"

"Apparently my dad wants to talk to me," he replied, avoiding the question—a typical Galician trait. "Don't make coffee for me. I´ll have some at home." A quick peck on the cheek and he was gone.

I looked at the three steaming cups of coffee in exasperation. "Oh, blow it!" I thought to myself and threw another couple of slices of buttered bread onto the hob. The instant burning smell of breadcrumb remnants cruelly reminded me of the earlier confrontation and seemed to mockingly highlight my position. I had definitely burnt my bridges with Pilar in regards to cooking.

Daniel returned an hour later and shouted up the stairs, "My dad wanted to know why I hadn't brought you with me this morning. He's invited you to the house for lunch." His smile waned as he entered the bedroom and realised that I´d taken myself back to bed and was lying despondently under the covers to keep warm.

"What are you doing? Get up, we'll go for a walk around the town and then we must be back at mum's for lunch at one o'clock."

* * * *

That afternoon, for the first time ever, I entered the inner sanctum of Pilar's domain: the kitchen. She stood at the stove, wrapped in a *delantal*, an apron splattered with various food stains that seemed to act as a status symbol. It openly signified her skill and expertise in the art of cooking whilst simultaneously further backing up my belief that my culinary attempts paled into insignificance. I wanted to dissolve into a puddle of water on the floor, like the wicked witch of the West, then ooze out of the door and discretely disappear like a Galician *bruja*.

Pilar worked with agility and competency as she spooned out a myriad of different dishes all at once; great platefuls of food with dietary differences for each male member of the family. Daniel, with his allergy to onion; Roberto who only ate the yolk of an egg; Ramón who only liked the albumen; and Miguel, who, for some reason, refused to eat meat and chips on the same plate. To add to the dietary complications, I did not eat meat. I spied a small frying pan with a piece of fish sizzling lightly and deduced that was for me.

We (the children) sat patiently at the table, waiting to be served. Pilar placed a plate of food in front of each of us with reverence and a contented expression on her face. Her sons immediately tucked in—all except one, Javier.

"Mamá, not green beans again!" He groaned, dramatically holding his head in his hand when he saw the dollop of *judías* sitting on his plate.

I glanced at Daniel for an explanation.

"Dad has several parcels of land where he grows corn. My mum always plants green beans at the same time, so that they will grow up the corn shoots and won't need any extra support."

"Yeah, so as you can imagine, we have a lot of corn and a never-ending supply of bloody judías," Javier joined in. "They are, apparently, a staple, dietary part of this household."

Pilar clipped him lightly behind the head with her wooden spoon. "Don't start, there's nothing wrong with green beans!"

Javier acquiesced and dug his fork into the mound of greenery with a sigh.

The kitchen door opened and in walked Javier senior. Removing his cap, he grinned sheepishly at his wife. "I'm home."

"Where have you been? Lunch has been ready for ten minutes," Pilar said, brandishing the spoon in his direction and carelessly depositing a blob of sauce on the kitchen floor.

"I got talking in the bar and I couldn't get away."

Pilar turned back to the stove, shaking her head and muttering to herself about tardiness and bad manners, as she began to dole food onto her husband's plate. Javier senior smiled as he sat down. He had an air of serenity about him that was attractive. He was the real boss of the household, but in the kitchen he let Pilar reign.

Ramón left the table and went to the heavy wooden plate drainer on the kitchen wall to retrieve a *cunca*, a white earthenware bowl, which his father filled with homemade Albariño wine and sipped throughout the meal. When the obligatory salad in the middle of the table had been devoured along with copious amounts of bread, the wine had been imbibed, and all the plates were empty, the fruit bowl was passed around. I soon learnt that kiwis were also in endless supply as they too grew in the garden's huerta.

After showing my surprise, I was ushered out of the kitchen by Daniel and Ramón, who took me down to visit the birthplace of my kiwi. The two plants, one male and one female— the mummy and daddy of the half-eaten kiwi I held guiltily in my hand—were so well-established that the fruit hung down in heavy clusters, bending the woody vines with the weight of the succulent fruit. The plants (more like trees) were growing alongside the accompanying Albariño grapevines on the typical construction of cemented pillars topped with crisscrossed wiring. The Albariño grapes occupied the majority of the huerta, and, as it was

September, the fruit was also in abundance. Ramón reached up and carefully picked a bunch for me to try.

"These vines are part of a cooperative," he explained. "My father sells the grapes to a bottling company every year. The cooperative test the grapes for their alcoholic content and tell us exactly when they must be picked."

"Interesting," I replied, thinking it would be quite a job to pick the overabundance of fruit.

Strategically placed around the rest of the huerta were several other well-established trees, from which I was able to deduce most of the other fruit we had been eating had originated. On the ground, dotted in several different areas, was a plethora of home-grown produce flourishing in the soil: lettuce, tomatoes, onions, carrots, cabbage, pumpkins, and the local *grelos*, or turnip greens, used in the typical Galician stews or casseroles (*estofados* and *guisos*). The deep, richly tilled soil of Galicia crumbled underfoot like black icing sugar—a stark difference from the hard-baked soil of the Murcia region where my attempts at gardening seemed pointless in comparison. I marvelled at the self-sufficiency I was witnessing.

* * * *

Over the following years, I sat at Pilar's table and savoured her entire repertoire of meals—all personally adapted for my vegetarian tastes, even her excellent Cocido Gallego, which takes up to three days to prepare, was adapted. A poor pig's tongue, ears and shoulder are steeped in salt water for two days and then cooked slowly for hours. Chickpeas are soaked and cooked separately from the cabbage, potatoes, grelos, and potatoes. The pork, along with beef and chorizo, are served on one dish; the cabbage on another, a third for the remaining vegetables and potatoes, and a fourth for the chickpeas. (I ate the vegetables!)

Once, I asked her how to make Vieiras, the Galician scallops served in their shell and cooked in the oven with breadcrumbs and a generous measure of Albariño wine. Pilar had looked pleasantly surprised and pleased at my request for her recipe.

Two days later I was sent a message to be in the kitchen at eleven thirty sharp, where I would be made privy to her secret formula for fabulous Vieiras. I arrived feeling quite nervous, like a novice attending a Master Chef class and watched as she ran the scallops under the tap.

"This part you snip off," she explained, attacking the mollusc with a pair of kitchen scissors. "Then put them back in there." She pointed to a baking tray laden with empty shells. "These shells are a typical symbol associated with the Pilgrims' walk to Santiago de Compostela. Did you know that?"

I shook my head, "No."

"They were originally used to scoop water out of the rivers, to drink when walking the trail."

"Interesting."

"Yes. Now, chop up the onion."

"How much do I need?"

"*Pues, suficiente*," (well, sufficient.) "Then add the bread crumbs." She liberally sprinkled the pan rallado over each scallop as though she were sowing corn in the campo.

"How many grams do I need?"

"*Bueno, bastante.*" (Well, enough.)

"*Vale*," I replied, becoming more vexed by the minute.

"Then the wine, okay?" she said, staring at my bewildered expression with a hint of annoyance, probably feeling that she was totally wasting her time.

"How mu . . . ?"

"A moderate amount!" she snapped.

As she reached for the salt, I thought I'd know the correct answer.

"A pinch of salt," I said, and then wished I hadn't as a fistful of sea salt was tossed liberally over the Vieiras and half of the kitchen units.

"Then cook them." She shoved the tray into the oven.

Still trying to show interest, although I had long lost hope of ever being able to replicate the recipe, I asked my last question. "How long do we have to cook . . . ?"

"I´ve just got a new oven, we´ll have to wait and see," she interrupted.

Over the next half an hour, every male member of the family came to peer inside the oven and adjust the temperature. I was at a total loss!

"How will we know when they are ready?"

"You just know," Pilar replied, sighing with annoyance. "Now, when you get back to Murcia, you can practice, and when you can make them as well as me, you can cook them in my kitchen."

* * * *

Here I was, twenty years later, and I had finally made it. I was cooking in Pilar's inner domain, although I was there through sheer necessity rather than by royal appointment. I continued stirring the corn and beans, remembering the last twenty years. There had been marriages, births, and, unfortunately, last year the untimely death of my father-in-law, who had turned out to be the perfect *suegro* with a great sense of humour and was dearly missed.

As I continued to stir pots, flip fish, and check the roasting meat as though my life depended on it, I heard the doorbell ring and a sense of foreboding flashed before me as, once again, I reminisced about my toast debacle.

"No!" I thought aloud and headed for the front door, hoping to get rid of the caller as quickly as possible. I knew that the slightest lack of concentration on my part would almost certainly result in some sort of culinary disaster.

"There's a man looking at your grapes," the neighbour began, having omitted any form of friendly greeting when she found me answering the door.

"Err, What?"

"There's a man looking at your grapes," she repeated. "You and your husband did inherit the huerta, didn't you, when your father-in-law died?"

"Well, yes, but . . ."

"Well, hurry up then. Hurry up, he's down there now!"

My mind was racing. What did she mean by "a man was looking at the grapes"? Was he casing the joint with the intention of stealing them? I felt totally out of my depth.

"But I'm cooking lunch on the stove . . ."

21

"Leave it, leave it. This is far more important."

I ran to change my slippers for sturdier shoes and looked frantically around for a key to the front door.

"Never mind the key, just leave the door open. Nobody will come in here." Her scathing comment and disdainful glance around the dining room made me unsure as to her meaning. Either she thought there was nothing worthy of stealing, or she wished to portray that Meaño was still a town where neighbours could leave their doors open without the worry of being robbed. (I hoped it was the latter as my search for a key had been in vain.)

"Go, go, go!" The neighbour shooed me out of the kitchen with wafting hand movements, spurring me on like a trainer coaching a Marathon runner as I sprinted down towards the huerta. I rounded the corner at speed and crashed straight into the man in question. As we both extricated ourselves from each other and brushed ourselves down, I don´t know who was more startled.

"Who are you and what are you doing?" I said, sounding rather more abrupt than I had intended.

"I'm checking the grapes," He replied indignantly. "Who are you? And why do you want to know what I'm doing?"

I explained that my father-in-law had passed away and that my husband (and therefore, by default, me) were now the new owners of the huerta, so the grapes that he had been perusing were mine.

"Ah!" he said smiling, as recognition passed across his face. "Now I understand. You´re the English girl married to Daniel, no?"

I nodded.

"Every year your father-in-law sold his grapes to our company and I´m here now to tell you when to pick them," he said. "Come with me, I´ll explain exactly what I´m doing." He took my arm in an almost vicelike grip and marched me further into the huerta. As I glanced behind me the house grew smaller by the second and I imagined the lunch slowly cremating itself to death on the stove.

His free hand dug into his pocket and he pulled out a cylindrical, copper object reminiscent of a telescope. The end sloped away and held a flat, clear surface with a flap, which he now lifted up. He grabbed a grape from the vine and squeezed it onto the flat surface, trapping the juice by placing the top over it, rather like a slide in a microscope.

"*Mira*," he said, proffering the "telescope". "Look inside. There are two scales."

I squinted into the tube.

"On the right is the level of alcohol. On the left is the sugar level. Between twelve and fourteen is good. More than fifteen *es difícil*. What does it say?"

"Err . . . thirteen?"

"*Correcto*! In two days, you must *Vindimiar*." (After twenty years, I knew this meant that we had to harvest the grapes.)

He smiled and left, almost bowing as I sprinted back towards the house. Unbelievably, there was no smell of burning— which was a definite plus. Surprisingly, everything still appeared to be in an edible condition. Unfortunately, with the added stress, all of Pilar's instructions as to what foods had to be mixed with others had gone completely from my mind. I stood there in a pickle. It was ten to one and the hordes would be here any minute, so I made a rash decision.

"Oh, blow it!" I said and spooned each separate foodstuff into mismatched bowls and plates, lining them all up along the kitchen units. I set the table with the Albariño wine, serviettes, plates, cutlery, and bread. Then I stood back as the front door opened. In they marched. They came to a standstill, staring in surprise at the myriad of receptacles before them.

"It´s a buffet lunch!" I informed them, holding out my hand to present my culinary "masterpiece". There was an audible silence, but after a few seconds, they all shuffled towards the food and tucked in.

"This is actually a good idea!" Javier grinned, spooning corn onto his plate and purposely avoiding the beans.

Pilar nodded in my direction. "Not bad," she said, as I felt an overwhelming surge of pride. "The problem is that this way, there´ll be a lot of washing up, and of course," she smiled slyly, "I'm still waiting for your version of my Vieiras!"

To Be a Pilgrim . . .

Liza Grantham

(Third place Poetry 2019)

Bill Jones was a hiker who loved the outdoors.
He'd trekked over hillsides and mountains and moors.
This year he would try something daring and bold:
He'd walk the Camino like the pilgrims of old.

He'd carry a gourd and a staff and a shell,
And when he got home, oh, the stories he'd tell!
He'd fill up his gourd from the crystal-clear fountains
And fend off the wolves as he passed o'er the mountains.

He'd spend every night sleeping under the stars,
With no need for hotels or hostels or bars.
He'd be taking a compass, no need for the signs,
As he wove through the oak trees and chestnuts and pines.

He set out at daybreak, it brought him such pleasure
To wander through woodland and fields at his leisure.
He ambled so freely, didn't notice time passing,
'Til the sky became darker with rain clouds amassing.

The drizzle came first, then it started to pour,
And he sensed that he'd passed through this forest before.
He opened his compass with fingers now numb—
Sure enough he was walking the way that he'd come!

He'd been wandering around in a circle for hours,
Now perished and soaked from the terrible showers;
If the wolves didn't eat him he'd freeze on the ground
And it might be a year 'til his body was found!

24

He shivered and stumbled, his strength disappearing,
About to collapse when he came to a clearing
He could make out the roadside and lights from afar,
He dragged himself onwards and flagged down a car.

"Er, do you speak English? I can't find my way—
I'm meant to be heading for Palas de Rey!"
He felt such a fool 'cos his trek almost killed him—
Take heed if you've thoughts of becoming a pilgrim!

A Dream Comes True

Liza Grantham

(Third Place Prose Non Fiction 2019)

It is April, but the warmth of the evening sunshine belies the fact that it is only early spring: lizards dart in and out of crevices in the moss-covered stone wall; a blue tit clings deftly to a strand of swaying broom abundant with buds of yellow; bees hover over a mass of wild flowers beneath the fig tree; a swallow flutters out from the rafters of the barn, swooping, effortlessly, high into the clear blue sky; the soothing breeze, though gentle, stirs the apple trees decked in white blossom, yet the chestnut with its majestic strength remains still.

I shift my position on the gnarled oak trunk resting across a ridge of rocks that rises up above the grass and clover. Enchanted by the beauty and tranquillity that surrounds me, I reflect on the events of the past year: how the pursuit of a dream had turned into a nightmare and how that dream had finally come true.

* * * *

Only a year ago, whilst living in the Canary Islands, our first attempt to buy a house in Galicia had failed miserably: the sale had fallen through on the very day we were due to sign! All those hours spent scouring property Web sites, making phone calls, moving money, booking flights and hotels, not to mention months of working extra hours and saving determinedly—I was utterly devastated, convinced that our dream just wasn't meant to come true. Deflated and downhearted I accepted defeat, unable to contemplate the thought of beginning the whole process all over again. My husband, Gary, however, was insistent that we shouldn't give in. What had happened to my fighting spirit? Where was my sense of adventure? Did I really want to abandon our dream?

Eventually, I rallied round and, pushing my earlier resignation aside, I agreed to try again.

With renewed enthusiasm we threw ourselves back into our quest. Our original criteria remained unchanged—the house would need to have water, electricity, and sewerage; the walls and roof must be basically sound; it must have land attached, at the very least enough for a decent vegetable garden and a few chickens; it would stand on its own, with no close neighbours. In addition, I now insisted that viewings would be limited to houses with only one owner—our previous disaster had arisen because of a dispute between a family of nine! For over a week we scrolled through page after page of photographs and descriptions. Our attention kept returning to a house that we'd been interested in during our first round of searching but had rejected because it stood in a lane with other houses close by. Everything else about it seemed ideal:

A house with an extraordinary barn in a village close to Antas de Ulla. It has water, electrics and sewage. The lower floor is still in animal pens and kitchen. On the upper floor there is a complete bathroom, four bedrooms and a terrace. It has enough garden for a good vegetable patch . . .

Furthermore, it appeared from the photographs to be immediately habitable and the asking price was well within our budget. I suggested that perhaps an isolated spot wasn't necessary after all—indeed, as newcomers to the region and the lifestyle there would be a number of advantages to being part of a small community: the help and support of our neighbours, the benefit of local knowledge and experience, the pleasure of enjoying other company from time to time. We examined maps and guidebooks to find out more about the area. The location was perfect. Antas de Ulla was in the southwest corner of the Lugo Province, but only a short distance from the borders of the other three—A Coruña, Pontevedra, and Ourense—this was the very heart of Galicia! Excitedly, I called Mark, the estate agent, for more information.

"How many owners?" I asked him, already dreading his reply.

"Just the one," he answered.

"Are you sure?" I persisted, anxious not to repeat our previous experience.

"Positive," he assured me. "A girl from Pontevedra, keen for a quick sale. The paperwork's all ready, so if you were over for a few days we could sort out the signing before you flew back."

I grinned into the telephone.

"We'd like to come over at Easter to see it," I told him.

Mark would be taking a break on the coast with his family, but a Galician colleague who lived in the area would be happy to stand in. With a surge of excitement, I booked our flights for April.

* * * *

Maribel picked us up from the hotel at midday. Dressed simply but smartly in a dark suit and white shirt, she appeared professional yet unpretentious. She greeted us warmly and her cheerful manner put me instantly at ease. As the car drove out of the city, Maribel apologised for her lack of English and we exchanged pleasantries in Spanish to break the ice. The urban backdrop gradually gave way to a landscape bathed in green, and our small talk was soon replaced by easy conversation. After half an hour of light-hearted chatter and breathtaking scenery, signposts welcomed us into Monterroso, where Maribel told us she had lived for all of her life. On the outskirts of the town she slowed the car to a crawl and indicated her own house, a large stone building, immaculately restored. Once in the centre she pointed out various shops and amenities: the supermarket, an agricultural store, tool shops, a wood yard, a builder's merchant, the library, a leisure centre, and a square with a bandstand where fiestas were held in summer. Finally, she pulled up at her office to collect the keys to what we hoped would become our new home.

A short distance from Monterroso the road took us through Antas de Ulla, too small to be a town, yet to call it a village would, semantically speaking, be rather tenuous as it was hardly the picturesque setting that the term might suggest. Its original stone dwellings had been rudely infiltrated by grey concrete buildings, and garish plastic bar furniture sprawled into the main square, where bushes of rose and hibiscus were planted in lame apology. The overall impression was grim, but this would be our nearest access to basic supplies and essential services: a grocery store, a bakery, a butcher's shop, two or three café-bars, a garage, a post office, a medical centre and a public telephone. Six kilometres from Cutián, this would be our closest contact with civilisation!

With Antas behind us, we left the main road and drove deeper and deeper into the countryside, along a series of winding lanes that traced the undulating contours of the landscape. We gazed, spellbound, as a rich sylvan tapestry unfurled before us: valleys carpeted in rich green pasture and untamed meadows of rippling silver sedges; dense woodlands of oak and chestnut, their lustrous canopies announcing the arrival of spring. Along the roadside hedgerows of golden gorse and twisted bramble grew thickly over ancient walls of standing stones. We drove onwards, weaving from time to time through tiny *aldeas:* clusters of humble stone houses with wood smoke drifting from turreted chimneys, aged *horreos* on stilts of stone, and barns of roughly hewn chestnut and weathered rock. As we paused to allow the safe passage of a herd of orange cows, I watched a man with a mattock digging amongst rows of kale, while a woman in a chequered pinafore gathered armfuls of the huge green leaves.

Eventually, a rusting enamel signpost humbly announced our arrival in Cutián. On our left stood the tiny parish church of San Xoan, framed by rows of marble sepulchres and topped with a tarnished bell. To the right three cows grazed nonchalantly in the afternoon sun. We eased down towards a dozen or so houses scattered randomly on either side of a dusty lane, a few inhabited, the others long since abandoned. The lane narrowed and the car squeezed slowly around a final corner. I grabbed Gary's hand excitedly as we came to a halt in front of the house I recognised immediately from the photographs.

We stepped from the car and stood before a heavy green stable door, where Jesus welcomed us with outstretched hands, from a small enamel plaque. I held my breath as Maribel unlocked the door and pushed it open to reveal a wide entrance passage with whitewashed stone walls and a wooden ceiling with a splendid oak beam. Through a door on the right we entered a large kitchen, the layout of which was almost identical to that of the house we'd viewed previously: a central *cocina* surrounded on three sides by smooth marble surfaces with sturdy oak benches beneath; a low sink with marble draining boards; a dresser along one wall. With the April sunlight streaming in through the paned window the kitchen held instant charm: it was easy to imagine the smell of freshly baked bread on a summer morning or pots bubbling cheerily on a shiny black stove top as a cosy fire roaring beneath to warm the winter nights.

"It's gorgeous!" I breathed.

Back in the entrance passage, another door opened into a large storeroom where a further heavy ancient door swung open into animal pens sectioned off by enormous standing stones, the earthen floor still littered with straw. The pens covered the entire expanse of the ground floor, opening out onto the back of the lane.

Through a third door a wooden staircase led up into a spacious landing, warm from the sun which poured through two large windows facing the barn. This would make a bright, comfortable living area in the spring and summer months, I decided. In the far corner a door opened into the first bedroom, fully furnished, with a quaint recessed window which overlooked the garden. At the opposite end of the landing was a door to a second wide landing that stretched towards the back of the house, giving access to two more furnished bedrooms, each with its own peculiar feature, making them special in different ways. The first had an attractive exposed oak beam, which narrowed at one end before disappearing into the wooden cladding half way across the ceiling—a typical example of the higgledy-piggledy character of these old stone houses, built in such a seemingly ad hoc manner, yet remaining unshaken for almost two centuries!

The next bedroom had a rather fascinating cupboard with heavy chestnut doors built into an alcove in the deep stone wall. I wondered if it was concealing the entrance to a secret passage and couldn't resist opening a door to find out. I was puzzled to see a huge enamel pot full of something congealed and yellow which had seeped onto the shelf where it was sitting.

"Urgh!" I exclaimed. Gary and Maribel came over and peered in. Bravely I lifted the pot from the shelf and sniffed it cautiously. It was completely odourless which surprised me.

"Beeswax?" I suggested.

"It's *unto*," Maribel smiled, "Puts fat on your ribs to keep you warm in winter!"

I decided a thermal vest was a pleasanter option and hastily shoved it back into the cupboard.

At the end of the landing, a magnificent panelled door opened onto what had once been a typical open terrace spanning the width of the house, more recently converted into a smaller terrace with a bathroom and further bedroom to either side. In contrast to the rest of the house, this section would need some repair. Crude chipboard cladding hung crumbling from the beams and the whitewashed walls were blackened with mildew. We had to step carefully over parts of the floor which had succumbed to the elements over time. It was clear that it would be better to enclose the remaining terrace section completely, to keep the heat in and avoid further damage to the floor. We assessed the work involved and came to the conclusion that this section would need to be reroofed, but once this was completed and the terrace closed in, all in all it wouldn't be too pricy.

Apart from a thoroughly good cleaning and a few coats of paint, it was clear that the house needed little work to be instantly habitable. Furthermore, the bedrooms were completely furnished: the beds, wardrobes and bedside tables were all of superb quality and in good condition. What we'd seen so far delighted us and our enthusiasm was growing—we couldn't wait to see the garden and . . .

"The barn!" cried Gary, who'd been excited about it ever since we'd first read the Web site's description.

"Wait!" laughed Maribel, reaching above the backdoor where a big rusty key was hanging. "There's more!"

"More?" we echoed in unison. Compared to where we were currently living the house seemed huge—there couldn't be any more of it . . . could there? Sure enough, Maribel led us out into the lane, where she unlocked the door of an adjacent building, an annexe that had originally been accessed through the main house. Although the giant stone doorway had been filled in, to reopen it would be a simple task and the annexe could be transformed into a dining room with a further lounge area on the mezzanine above.

31

At last, Gary's wish was granted as we crossed the lane to the enormous two-storey barn that stood opposite the house. It certainly lived up to the Web site's description—it was, indeed, "extraordinary". It was typically Galician in that the north and east facing sides were of slatted chestnut, the other two of stone, but unusual in that it had been built into the rocky side of the steeply elevated garden. The ground floor was accessed from the lane, whilst a door on the upper floor opened directly into the garden.

Beside the barn, what appeared to be a wide overgrown sloping pathway, but which was, in fact, the original threshing floor, rose up to two giant stone tables. Beyond these, stretched a large grassy area overgrown with tall weeds and bracken—it would certainly need some tending before vegetables could be persuaded to grow there!

As we walked across the garden, Maribel stopped half way.

"This part wouldn't be yours," she informed us, indicating a strip of land five or six metres wide.

"What do you mean?" I asked, puzzled.

"It belongs to someone else," she explained.

"I see," I answered, not really seeing at all. I looked at Gary who was frowning—the thought of a stranger traipsing over our garden wasn't really what we had in mind.

"You'd be able to buy it cheaply, though," she went on, registering our obvious concern. "Maybe a thousand euros. The owner's very old and in a nursing home. She won't be coming back to Cutián." Whether due to her professional efficiency or simply as a result of access to the local grapevine, Maribel was clearly well-informed.

We continued to the end of the garden through a wall of standing stones into an area overgrown with bracken beneath the shade of a large chestnut tree.

"You could grow corn in this bit," she suggested, but I'd already decided it would be the perfect site for a chicken coop.

As we wandered back across the garden towards the lane, Gary and I discussed our impressions of the house. The kitchen and first floor were already habitable and partly furnished, and these alone would give us a generously sized home. In addition, the animal pens and galleried annexe offered the potential for other projects at a later date. The lower storey of the barn would serve as a workshop and log store whilst the upper level would make a shady relaxation area on summer evenings. The garden was bigger than we'd dared hope for, with the added bonus of fruit trees and an attractive patio area already in place. We were still concerned about the strip of land with the mysterious owner and once more sought Maribel's reassurance about its future sale. Satisfied that we could trust her word, it wasn't hard to make a decision.

"Well," smiled Gary "What do you think?"

"You *know* what I think," I beamed. "It's perfect!" This time there wasn't a single doubt in my mind.

We'd made our decision, and asked Maribel to put forward our offer as soon as possible. She promised to call that afternoon and, sure enough, within an hour of returning to our hotel in Lugo, my phone rang. Our offer had been accepted and we were to await further information about the signing.

"Can it be arranged for this week?" I asked excitedly.

"Oh yes, it'll probably be Tuesday or Wednesday," came the reply. "I'll call the *notario* tomorrow morning to make the appointment. I'll ring you as soon as I know."

My heart leapt with joy! At last I'd have my long-awaited farmhouse kitchen and Gary would have his barn! I'd be able to collect fresh eggs, gather greens like the woman in the pinafore, and. . . . Stop! I told myself, remembering that we had come this far before. I thought back to the first house once again: its bleak appearance from the roadside; the unwelcoming icy wind as we opened the door; the dingy kitchen that I'd struggled to imagine myself working in; the sizzling bare wire warning us to keep away. Today was a completely different experience—this house felt warm and welcoming, as though it was holding cherished memories within its walls. Something told me that this time nothing would shatter the dream.

On Tuesday morning we set out, more than a little apprehensively, for our appointment with the *notario*. As we turned into Rúa da Raiña I tried to brush aside the memory of our previous ill-fated visit, but the scene was all too familiar: the shops, the kiosks, the cafes, the milling crowds—even the timing of our appointment was exactly the same! At that moment I spotted Maribel waving from the entrance to the mall. The sight of her was reassuring and I quickly regained my composure.

"Mónica's already here," she announced brightly, as we hastened our pace to greet her. We exchanged kisses. "She's in the waiting room upstairs."

We climbed a wide staircase to the second floor and entered a busy reception area with a small waiting room to the side. On a table in the corner, next to the ubiquitous pile of magazines, a basket of boiled sweets seemed ominously to suggest that we might be there for some time. A young woman clutching a plastic document wallet smiled and rose from her seat as we entered. Maribel introduced us before heading to the reception desk to inform them that we were all present. Mónica was chatty and friendly, and although my nervousness had left me unusually reluctant to engage in conversation, I joined in with Gary, asking about the house and the *aldea*. We learned that the house had belonged to her grandfather and, although there were other grandchildren, he had left her the house because she was the only girl. She and her husband had a large, modern apartment in Vigo, and whilst she had happy memories of the time she'd spent in the house as a child, she had no reason to hang on to it. She was expecting her first baby at the end of summer, so the money from the sale would be very welcome. She assured us that the neighbours were nice people who'd help us out if the need arose. Maribel returned from reception and, to excuse myself from further conversation, I feigned interest in a set of tastefully framed watercolours depicting facets of the cathedral. Maribel and Mónica chatted amicably in Galician, pausing only occasionally to help themselves to sweets. Maribel gestured me to take one, but I declined.

"But you *must*," she insisted. "They're *free!*"

Just then, a tall man appeared in the doorway, officious in manner yet casually dressed in jeans. He beckoned us to follow and ushered us into a conference room, dominated by a long wooden table and ten or more rather uncomfortable-looking chairs. More baskets of sweets were situated centrally and I couldn't help but notice a further supply on top of a filing cabinet by the window. Their presence did little to lessen the formality of our surroundings and I hoped nervously that the process would be quick. The man introduced himself as Luis, stated the purpose of our meeting, and asked for our identity documents. As he read our names aloud we each nodded in confirmation. Then he left the room to make photocopies. Maribel unwrapped a sweet and pushed the basket towards me.

"The *notario* is very rich," she chuckled, winking, "Eat as many as you can!"

I laughed, and took one because there seemed to be little else to do. After a few minutes Luis returned. This time he asked Mónica for the surveyor's report and read a description of the property: "A house in the municipality of Antas de Ulla . . ." We all nodded in agreement again and Luis left for further photocopying. was apparently required, this time it took much longer. Next came the deeds of sale, this time a lengthy document with lots of legal jargon "a two-storey house . . ." We nodded again and Luis disappeared. The ritual of reading, nodding, and photocopying continued for half an hour, interspersed with much sucking and crunching of sweets. At last, it was time to bring proceedings to a close, and the *notario*, Jose Antonio, entered the room. Immaculately dressed in a well-cut suit and tie, He bore a distinct air of importance and his size suggested he was no stranger to the gastronomic delights of the region. After a brisk introduction he read rapidly through the sheaf of papers before scribbling a flourish with an elegant ballpoint on the final page. Mónica, Gary, and I added our own signatures, this time with cheap plastic biros produced by Luis. Jose Antonio shook our hands and departed, followed by Luis for one last trip to the photocopier. Gary handed Mónica a bulging envelope and she counted its contents, note by note, onto the polished table. I took a sweet and crunched nervously until, eventually, she smiled and nodded, satisfied that it was correct. A wave of sheer relief washed over me and everyone laughed as I let out a loud heartfelt sigh. Maribel handed Gary the keys, Luis returned with copies of the documentation, we exchanged thanks and good wishes and said our goodbyes. After more than an hour (or, as we later joked, almost three baskets worth of boiled sweets) the ordeal was over. Out in the street Gary and I lit cigarettes, long overdue, and we beamed delightedly as we headed for the nearest bar, knowing that at last our dream had come true.

Hyenas? Never!

Liza Grantham

(Honourable Mention Poetry 2019)

My new English neighbour looked troubled.
"What's happened?" I asked, and he frowned.
"This might sound a really daft question,
But are there hyenas around?

"I know I don't speak any Spanish,
But I saw Carmen out in the lane;
As she chattered away I could make out one word:
Hyenas—again and again!"

I chuckled and said, "No, of course not!
There are roe deer and wolves and wild boar . . ."
"She must have been pulling my leg then,
'Cos the word was hyenas, I'm sure."

I saw Carmen out in her garden.
Excited, she called through the fence;
She'd bought some new hens from the market—
Now the puzzle began to make sense . . .

My neighbour, of course, was mistaken.
Hyenas, that wasn't the word!
She'd been talking nonstop about chickens,
And it was *gallinas* he'd heard!"

Language Barriers

Lisa Wright

As an émigré, I cannot overemphasize the importance of learning the language of ones adopted country—not just to be able to order a beer or book a hotel room but also to foster communication, which is essential to get into the psyche of a community and to begin to integrate and to truly understand the place you have chosen to live.

Unfortunately, we English, as a race, are particularly poor at learning languages. Instead, we expect Johnny foreigner to understand English as the *lingua franca* of the civilised world. Be warned, in rural Galicia this is not the case. The second language of most of our neighbours is Castilian, *Galego* being the first and most important language.

Our neighbour does, however, have a very English way of trying to make the stupid foreigners understand. She comes to within one inch of my left ear and shouts in that wonderfully carrying, piercing cry she uses to summon the cows from across the valley. Sadly, the overall result of this method of knocking the language into me has the entirely opposite effect, literally blowing the vestiges of any language out of my right ear and away across the fields, leaving me open mouthed, deaf, and temporarily incapacitated and reinforcing the belief that these *extranjeros* are *tonto* and unable to understand simple questions.

This belief was, in any case, planted firmly in the collective consciousness of the village one day early in our three-month sojourn to Galicia and shortly after we had found the beautiful, derelict, and neglected stone *casa* that was to become our home.

We had been visiting the house, clearing the myriad of ancient bills (mainly unpaid), blister packs of pills (for conditions both human and animal), and old X-rays (of every conceivable part of the body . . . probably human) when an outrider in the form of an elderly lady on two sticks arrived to measure our worth as new neighbours.

Whether our visitor was chosen as elder of the village or as an acceptable sacrifice should we prove hostile (after all we were the first *extranjeros* to be seen in the village . . . foreigners not being widespread in these parts) and what words of welcome she intended to convey we shall never know as I had chosen the precise moment of her arrival to commune with some bees in the lower field, so I missed the entire exchange.

The following, therefore, is carefully transcribed from the notes Ambassador S made at the time whilst holding the banner for Britannica on this solemn and important occasion.

Visitor: (marching forward with remarkable speed on two crutches) gabble, gabble, gabble.

S: (at a loss) Erm.

Visitor: gabble, gabble.

S: *No entiendo* (or no Nintendo, as one particular Brit insisted on saying).

Visitor: gabble, gabble.

S: (shouting in the direction of the woods) Lisa!

Visitor: gabble, gabble?

S: (increasingly frantic) Lisa! Er, *mi mujer*, (pointing to the woods).

Visitor: (comprehending) *No hablas Galego*? No problem I'll switch to Castilian.

S: (mumbling) Great I still don't understand a word.

This "conversation" continued for a brief while longer in the same vein until our visitor finally wandered away to muse on the eccentricities of the odd, but probably harmless *Ingleses,* who wave their arms around, shout into thin air, and make no sense at all.

La Santa Compaña

Jennifer Juan

I saw my heart,
moodily moving,
grieving in glorious white,
a hood to hide her tears,
as she joined La Santa Compaña.

I could taste my heart's torment,
as I stood,
open mouthed,
watching the wounds I left,
lit up by the candle she proudly held.

Melted wax met my senses,
sending me back,
to the many times I had broken her,
bringing her to this place,
with my careless sharing of her.

The living leader may not remember,
but I will struggle to forget,
cursed to regret,
as I take up the cauldron and cross,
to lead in his place.

Chick, Chick, Chick, Chick Chicken

Lisa Wright

(Second Place Prose Non Fiction 2019)

Chick, chick, chick, chicken, lay a little egg for me, I haven't had one since Easter and now it's half past three . . .

This silly childhood ditty had been going round and round in my head for days. I knew why. It *was*, in fact; Easter, we had had our first ever chickens for almost three weeks; and we had yet to be presented with a single, solitary egg!

One of the big draws of Galicia other than the cost of living, and let's not beat about the bush, cost is a big factor in the choice of a good life venue whatever excuses we make, was the ability to be able to afford (see, I told you . . . cost) enough land with a nice derelict house on it to be self-sufficient to some degree.

Being me, and being exceptionally careful when it comes to planning, I had extensively researched what was required. How many potatoes needed to be planted for two people for a year, how many cabbages, how much corn for the chickens, how many trees to provide firewood, etc., etc. I filled pages and pages of my notebooks. It appeared that three hectares was the target to be completely self-sufficient, so we started looking for properties with that amount of land. Let me tell you, that is a Lot of Land! Forget football pitches and other useless comparisons, it's just a lot. A lot to weed, a lot to sow, a lot to harvest, a lot to dig, and a lot to care for.

We regrouped, realising that we wouldn't have the time to properly look after so much land and to renovate a house, which we both wanted and needed to do to keep in budget. (Money again). Three hectares would basically be a small holding. For instance, if we grew wheat we would also have to harvest and mill it. If we had cows, we would have to put them to a bull or use artificial insemination (more cost); to milk them, and to have them slaughtered. Sheep escape, goats eat everything, and pigs?

Well, we saw a lovely sow at the local farmer's market. She was huge and white and we soon realised that if, come killing day, she didn't want to participate, we would struggle to convince her. As we stood admiring her chunky 200-pound figure, her statuesque 10-foot length, and her lovely big teeth, we caught each other's eyes and I had a vivid picture form . . . S approaching her on *matanza* day, the heavy wooden "pig killer" in his hand; me approaching from the other side with a bucket of food, wheedling, hemming her in. The sow watching us balefully with those little piggy eyes and . . . charging. The food scattering as I run. S manfully standing his ground woodworm old mallet in his raised hand before . . .

No, cross pigs off the list too.

So, we set our sights lower. Grow enough vegetables, fruit, and nuts to sustain us year round. Raise chickens and rabbits and buy a pig from our friend and neighbour. Not exactly self-sufficiency but a reasonable compromise.

Chickens were always one of our must haves for our new life. One can't, after all, live the good life without chickens! The garden chicken boom was just starting in the UK when we left and trendy, designer chicken houses could be had for less than 2,000 pounds. Mum regularly sent us lovely photos of them from the newspaper. One was a modern work of art. An egg-shaped hen house measuring two foot high by around a foot diameter. Apparently suitable for three hens, it looked both impossible to clean and totally impractical. It also seemed a perfect shape for a fox to roll away for a late-night snack. Our chooks would have an old brick, and inexpertly rendered, chicken shed, with wonderfully quirky Galician perches; long pieces of thick tree branch sitting on four splayed legs at just the right height above the floor. And all for free!

I read up on chicken care: what to feed and when, what to look for and at what age I would get that all important first egg. I read stories glorying in incompetency: of foxes taking hens at night because the hen house door was left open; of going away for weekends and forgetting to feed the hens. I read up on expert advice telling me that hens will only lay when there are more than fourteen hours of daylight and need artificial lighting in winter if one wants year-round eggs (no one told ours) and accounts from friends saying you can just throw a few scraps at them and get ten eggs a day (no one told ours that either).

In fact. all my reading and research prepared me not one jot for the arrival of our first three point-of-lay brown pullets.

We decided, in the interests of being able to eat them if necessary, not to give the chickens names but numbers. One, two and three had captain, sergeant, and corporal stripes on their legs to identify them. The numbers lasted about as long as the felt tip stripes. Number two became the very un-PC Fatty due to her habit of eating anything in sight. A slowworm, which we managed to pull out of her gullet alive if a little bemused; a mouse, which had the misfortune to run into the pen . . . I still don't know how she managed the bones, but it disappeared down there somehow . . . and my fingers at every opportunity. Number three was a spectacular jumper, managing to raise herself a good three feet (that's a metre for the youngsters out there) from a standing start, especially if this meant she could reach the grape vines that we had thoughtfully provided for shade over the summer. So full of grapes was she that her name became Veronique after the chicken dish of the same name. And number one, was and always will be, Number One.

Rural *Galegos* in general have a different attitude to animals than the squeamish British. We feel it is barbaric to kill an animal for food whilst happily buying some packaged piece of water-filled cardboard on sale at 1.99 down the supermarket. There are still many of our friends who can't believe we really kill things, though they themselves are far from being vegetarians. Our neighbours keep animals for food and for necessity. They are looked after accordingly and killed when needed. Although not animal lovers, in the sense of keeping animals as pampered pets, our neighbours are not without feelings for their livestock.

One day our neighbour Carmen came to the allotment where I was working. She slapped a chicken onto the granite step and called "*Mira*! Look at this". Taking in the situation at a glance I realised the chicken was dead. It wasn't difficult; it had no head!

"The third this week, what are we going to do?"

We decided to set up a trap, guessing from the bite marks that the perpetrator was a weasel or pine marten. I duly went to an agricultural supplier and explained the problem to the young female assistant.

Her eyes grew round as she blurted out "I know what that is!" She said something in *Galego*. "Oh yes! Farmers have many problems with them taking the milk of a cow"

"Really? But how is it called in Castilian?"

"Oh, they are only in Galicia. They have much danger to chickens"

I wrote down the *Galegan* name and showed it to Carmen when I delivered the trap. She looked bemused and shook her head.

"What is it?"

"Small animal, spiky, many times is run over"

Ah! That will be that well-known felon, the ninja hedgehog, then!

Although we never did catch the chicken killer, an RSPCA inspector friend later told me a gruesome story of finding a hedgehog devouring a litter of new-born, abandoned kittens, so maybe they are not as harmless as we both thought as we shared a smile that spring day.

Our main pest, or eater of chickens, we found to be the beautiful but deadly buzzard. This killer soars on thermals many metres above the chicken run and then plummets silently to snatch a meal. Chickens are not the smartest birds in the avian world and will often watch as the buzzard tears into their fallen comrade instead of running as fast as their little legs will go!

Our chickens started as free range. Then, as my flowers started to disappear, we put up a one-metre fence. They jumped it. Two-metre fencing followed, but this didn't stop the aerial attacks. We bought nylon wide-mesh netting for the top, which worked until a goshawk managed to dive straight through the mesh, taking poor Danni on the very day she laid her first egg. The mesh became chicken wire, which then had to be propped up, which then became a full construction project running into hundreds of euros to the amazement of our neighbours, who told us that chickens only cost seven euros at the market. True enough, but despite the fact that we would one day eat at least some of them, we didn't want someone else to do so! We felt we were losing the war, though we have had one triumph over the buzzard . . .

One sunny morning we were enjoying our cuppa on the terrace when S gave a shout. As I looked up, I caught sight of a shape near the chicken run. A cat? It took off. Not a cat then. We had chicks at the time, only six weeks old and still wandering about the garden. I screamed as the shape manifested itself into a deadly buzzard and ran down the path waving my arms frantically.

"Did it get one, did it get one?" I burbled. S thought so and a quick head count confirmed we were a chick down. Too late we herded the remaining babies inside and closed the pop hole.

Next morning I was in the pen when I saw a movement under the bramble bushes. Closer investigation showed it to be a small, dishevelled, shivering chick. S offered it a handful of corn, which it hoovered up in record time. Nothing puts a chick off its food for long. It seemed none the worse for wear, though one leg wasn't working properly. We pieced together events as best we could.

The buzzard, I still maintain due to my screaming (I can scream really rather well) and arm windmilling, must have dropped his prize as he flew away and Lucky, as the chick obviously became known, would have hidden in the bramble patch until hunger won out over fear.

We think the leg was damaged in the fall but however his injury came about, he needed help getting into the chicken pen for a few days but had no lasting problems—other than a tendency to boast about his fight with a monster to anyone who would listen!

Score one to us!

Shortly after we got our three browns we were given a cockerel and two further hens by an English friend. Buzz Lightyear and Sarah Bernhardt, his beautiful white Wyandotte wife, were to become the patriarch and matriarch of our vast chicken family in years to come.

And the second hen? Well, she turned out to be a he. Chicken sexing is notoriously difficult and years later I still wait for that first egg from the madly cockle doodle dooing hen I'm sure I've raised. Just as I was waiting that first Easter morning when I heard a mad clucking and shouting from the hen house. Running in I found a still warm and perfectly shaped brown egg in the straw and a triumphant if somewhat noisy hen strutting around the place calling, "I've done it, I've done it" over and over.

One egg is good. Now, just one more and we can have eggs for tea . . . chick chick chick chick chicken, lay a little egg for me . . .

Paradela

Dawn Hawkins

(Second Place Winner Poetry 2019)

On Monday, Paradela
is a sleepy little town.

On Tuesday, Paradela
has nothing going Down.

On Wednesday in Paradela,
you can buy yourself a cow.

On Thursday, Paradela
has a different feeling now.

In a square just off the main street
someone's setting up a Fair.
There's a sign up on the market
saying 'pedestrians beware'.
And just beyond the town
a closer look reveals
A farmer on his tractor
doing wheelies in his fields.

On Friday, Paradela
is getting very weird,
There's a ramp, a row of buses
And a lot of men with Beards.

On Saturday, Paradela
is a very different place.
Bikers clad in leather
are filling every space.

There are Hondas in the market place.
Ducatis in the park.
And as for Kawasaki,
they have built themselves an ark.
Yamahas are roaring
and drowning out the Sound
Of a leather cladded DJ
on Benelli sponsored ground.
He is playing heavy metal
to the Royal Enfield crowd.
While new models from Suzuki
will make their owners proud.
There's a stylish BMW,
An antique Norton too,
And a row of ancient Triumphs
that served in World War Two.
In pride of place on main-street
is Harley Davidson,
each one so well polished
they outshine the blazing sun.

On Sunday, Paradela
is a town gone slightly barmy,
With stuntmen jumping buses
and a display team from the army.
The market hall's a restaurant
behind a giant bar
So the locals are as happy
as the people from afar.

On Monday, Paradela
is a sleepy little town.
Just a few exhausted locals
taking all the posters down.

The Chimney Fire

Dawn Hawkins

(First Place Prose Non Fiction 2019)

Life is slow here in rural Galicia. A loose cow wandering onto the road, and thus delaying the bread van, is exciting enough to cause palpitations. Passing gypsies (allegedly) stole a dead and horribly corroded forty-year-old tractor battery, and it is still a hot topic of conversation some seven years after the event.

Deliveries can take weeks and are unpredictable. Sometimes it depends on whether the delivery person happens to be passing. The owner of the builder's yard delivers bricks on the way to church; firewood appears in the drive months after, and once or twice in anticipation of, an order. Messages regarding tradespeople can come via the baker, a neighbour, or the local bar. Our post is sometimes delivered to the butcher's shop in town because the butcher lives nearby, and we can find our parcels in the petrol station, cafe, or walking shop. This means that everyone knows if you have bought a new bed, or are working on the house, or even if you have visitors. There is very little that happens in a parish that does not become common knowledge before the day is out.

Fires, by contrast, are treated with urgency, the fire brigade responds quickly, and anyone nearby also rushes to help. We live in a land of forests with mild, wet winters encouraging undergrowth and hot, dry summers turning the undergrowth into bone dry tinder, making forest fires inevitable. There is a loss of life, livestock, and valuable timber as the tragic result.

Sometimes fires are dealt with quickly. The fire brigade and the neighbours all rush to help, not knowing how bad things are. Everyone feels a surge of adrenaline until they are sure that neither lives nor livestock are in danger because putting out any fire is dangerous. The adrenaline rush is followed by relief that no one is hurt. The results of this emotional roller coaster can be

48

comic, leading to a strange, almost party-like, atmosphere. A bit like singing in the rain. There was one such occasion in our village.

Our village has only six houses and fewer than twelve residents, but like most farming villages, it still follows the rhythm of the seasons. As summer cools and turns to autumn, cook stoves are cleaned out and the familiar smell of wood smoke fills the evening air. This particular evening, the first cold night of the autumn, we had guests staying. We had enjoyed a pleasant evening of wine and conversation before going upstairs to bed. Our guests had the bedroom on the village side of the house, whilst we slept at the back, facing away from the village. Had it not been for them, we might have missed all the excitement. We woke to Helen, our friend, banging on our bedroom door and shouting, "There is a fire engine outside our window. We need to find out where the fire is." Panic tinged her voice.

We dutifully threw on dressing gowns and rushed downstairs to join Paul, who was already checking the kitchen. Thankfully, he hadn't found anything to suggest fire, no smoke or falling beams, and the remaining coals in our stove were still in the firebox. The kitchen window, however, looks out at the centre of the village. People were milling around everywhere and in the strangest combination of clothes, almost like the set for a zombie film. Pyjamas with Wellington boots, coats, over nightdresses and slippers, pyjama bottoms with thick sweaters, boots with no socks, quite a crowd of strangely dressed people. More people were gathered than actually live in the village; a gathering of this size is normally reserved for a funeral or a fiesta. I quickly checked the calendar provided by the local baker that obligingly marks local fiestas. Nothing. No midnight pyjama party, Zombie gatherings, or midnight fundraisers for the firemen. Nothing on the calendar at all for today. So, not a fiesta then. We decided to swap our dressing gowns for coats and join the crowd, thinking we might be able to help. Why we bothered to change, I'm not sure, we would have blended better in our dressing gowns.

Our first difficulty was squeezing past the fire engine, which was wedged rather than parked outside our door. As we got to the front of the house and reached the crowd, a shower of sparks shot out of the chimney at Number 4. The fire men had unrolled their hose and had a ladder leaning on the roof, so we guessed that a chimney fire had caused the problem. The gates at Number 4 were open, and the men had started to organise a chain of buckets to throw water on the back of the roof and the barn to stop the fire spreading. This involved a lot of shouting. Gallego is a very versatile language, lending itself to poetry and song, but, I have to admit, it also lends itself to shouting, especially when something is being organised. It's rare that a conversation happens in the village street that we don't hear. Besides the shouting, the air was full of laughter and bottles of something (surely containing flammable liquids) being passed from hand to hand. The women, not to be outdone by the men, armed themselves with mops, buckets, and coffee pots. One of the neighbours sent me home to bring more cups. She seemed quite pleased with the size of the crowd.

On my return to Number 4, the scene had moved on from strange and was becoming surreal. The kitchen, a traditionally Galician farm kitchen, is large, with the wood stove set into the central island and a bench at the back. It was packed with people; two firemen were trying to pour what looked like damp sand into the wood stove to put it out. An elderly neighbour in her night clothes and a wraparound polyester overall and holding two large coffee pots batted them away so that she could use the still-lit stove to make coffee. Several more women had armed themselves with mops to try to stop black water spreading through the house. The water bubbled up from the cleaning vent in the stove's flue, which runs under the kitchen floor. Trying to contain the black water was a thankless task, as there were still two firemen on the roof with a hose sending water down the chimney in the direction of that very flue. Paca, whose house we were in, was in tears and being comforted with a large glass of brandy. In spite of this, cups of insanely strong coffee made on the electric "summer stove" were being passed in a chain to anyone who would take one. The cups then were being laced liberally with home-distilled aguardiente supplied by another neighbour.

Once the immediate danger to lives and homes had past, the atmosphere outside became more and more festive. The fire itself had been put out with commendable speed. What work remained was to make sure that it wouldn't restart. The house and adjoining barn had to be checked for sparks or embers and both needed to be cool and damp enough to discourage any smouldering material. The activity was great fun, and most of the men were also becoming damp, as the majority of the water failed to hit its intended target. Out of the corner of my eye I caught sight of a bedraggled and wet mother hen desperately trying to herd a group of chicks to a safer place, and one or two cats also wet and woken from sleep.

The fire box in the cooker was filled with damp sand so that it could not relight. This was achieved by the bravery of a firefighter who was prepared to work in a kitchen full of elderly Galician women. In my opinion, anyone taking a stand against an elderly woman in a polyester wrap armed with heavy metal coffee pots deserves recognition. The chimney would need cleaning and repairing before it could be used again. The men with the buckets were extremely cheerful, having obviously arrived in the village armed with a-little-something to keep them warm and cheerful. Any that hadn't were freely encouraged to share with those who had. This included the local police, whose arrival in a minivan seemed to me at the time like overkill, though no one else thought it remarkable. My neighbours, it transpired later, were right; the police were proved to be invaluable.

My nice, reserved, very English guests were standing to one side, each armed with an alcohol- and sugar-laced mug of espresso-strength coffee They wore matching striped pyjama bottoms visible beneath matching Goretex walking jackets. I wondered for a moment if I should warn them that the aguardiente, which I guessed had been distilled in our neighbour's shed, could easily be twice the strength of that from a shop. Or that the coffee was strong enough to be on the controlled substance list in the UK. The combination of the two has been known to have an alarming affect on anyone who hasn't had a lifetime to get used to it. A glance at their faces convinced me that they needed something to serve as shock treatment, and a caffeine, sugar, alcohol hit might prove to be necessary first aid.

The local police were needed in the end, because the new fire engine was firmly wedged in the lane outside our gate. The fire chief wasn't going to risk it being scratched for the sake of a mere chimney fire. So, there was no way he would drive forward into the narrowest part of the village, despite being assured that there was plenty of room by my, now cheerfully optimistic, neighbours. The many cars that had followed it in to the village had completely blocked the road and fire chief's exit, so at the moment he couldn't back out either.

It turned out to be a blessing to have half a dozen police officers available to direct traffic and to saw branches off the enormous walnut tree that overhangs the lane. They were able to get cars moving and clear enough space for the fire engine to be eased out backwards. It was three o'clock in the morning and everyone was just intoxicated enough to have loudly expressed opinions, and in case you are in any doubt, everyone had an opinion and expressed that opinion, more than once. We were more than happy to have police help.

I'm not sure that our guests have ever fully recovered from their visit. They went silently and not very steadily to bed that night. They certainly haven't been back, and before they left, they informed us in hushed tones how much they respected our bravery in coming here. The village recovered as soon as everyone left. The next day Paca got her chimney cleaned and had plenty of help to clean the mess the fire made. We returned to our sleepy lives. Fires are still treated with respect and chimney cleaning has become a higher priority, and for a while the local sweep was fully employed. He was able to enjoy a winter holiday on the islands with his family that year.

We know we got away lightly. Things could have been so much worse. Perhaps that's why the fire in our village is rarely remembered anywhere in the district without a smile.

Galician Mist

Dawn Hawkins

(First Place Poetry 2019)

It covers over mountain tops
and hides the rolling hills.
And winds its way up rivers
dimming swirls and rills.

It dances through the forest
with the spirits of the trees
And hides the fields and hedgerows
then hovers on the breeze.

On the lake it sunbathes,
with feathered falling motion
Yet settles in the valleys
Like a liquid silver ocean.

It mingles in the churchyard
with souls of the long gone,
then frightens playing children
With a half-heard mournful song.

Inhabits ruined cottages
with smoke from empty grates.
And grasps at passing pilgrims
With icy fingered fate.

It touches all the spider webs,
makes crystal chandeliers,
But in its passing over
leaves a washing lines of tears.

Legends ghosts and fairies
all hide within its folds.
But so do prayers of pilgrims
and the love of long lost souls.

That is why my homeland
by strangers is dismissed.
Because the heart of My Galicia
Is hidden in the mist.

Jo's Journey

Dawn Hawkins

(First Place Prose Fiction 2019)

I sit in my solicitor's office and stare at him blankly. He has been talking for a good five minutes and he had lost me after the first sentence. Our fathers had been school friends, so we grew up knowing each other. He has a kind, lived-in face. His suit is a little old and unfashionable and his office is above a newsagent. His other clients are refugees, single mothers, and the victims of abuse. Conveyancing, making wills, and the odd divorce pay the bills. He grabs my hand to get my attention. "Jo, what do you think?"

I stammer a little; I don't understand. "Someone has left me a house?" I query.

"Well, no, not exactly. It's more like a job with a house attached."

"And it's in this Galicia place?"

"Northwest Spain, just above Portugal." He draws a map in the air, as if it will help. There is a pause while he takes a deep breath, summoning up enough courage to continue. "Look, Jo, be honest. Tom's gone and he isn't coming back. The house will go too, even if Tom agreed, you can't afford to buy his share. What about your future? You must think about what's best for you."

That awful suffocating pain in my chest is back, my eyes fill with tears, and my head throbs. I need to get out. I 'don't want to hear this now. I want my life back.

I don't remember the journey home. I must have poured a glass of wine and cried myself to sleep on the sofa. I wake with a start, feeling stiff and sore, my mouth sandy. My phone is ringing; it's my manager from work pointing out that I should have been there three hours ago. I can't think of anything to say, so I put the phone down on the table and let him rant. I put the kettle on, and when I come back, he's gone.

I sip my tea and feel strangely calm; The words of a hymn come unbidden to my mind.

One day at a time, sweet Jesus
That's all I'm asking of you.
Just give me the strength to do every day what I have to do.
Yesterday's gone, sweet Jesus
And tomorrow may never be mine
Lord, help me today, show me the way one day at a time.

In my mind, the word "day" changes to "thing." Surely I can manage one thing. For the first time in months, there seems to be less fog in my head. I glimpse myself in the mirror and realise today's "thing" might be a shower and clean clothes. I repeat "clean and tidy" over and over in my head. I wash my hair, trim my fringe, sort clean clothes from dirty ones, clean my teeth, and look in the mirror again. I look tired, even ill, but I look respectable. I make lunch, clean the fridge, and make a shopping list.

Then on a whim I reach for my tablet and look up Galicia. The photos that appear are nothing like the Spain of my imagination, the Spain on the TV, and not like the Spain of my memories of Benidorm. I see castles and waterfalls, forests and pastureland. Impossible vineyards on the slopes of canyons and windswept beaches. There are pretty little coves, weathered granite villages, and medieval cities.

I think of the home I'm losing and my job, which I may well have lost. I think of my husband, whom I apparently still don't know after thirty years. Then I think of his solicitor with designer suits, too-white teeth, and predator's eyes. I realise the things I have lost are already gone. A bloody battle won't regain anything and might mean forcing the children to take sides. I make my mind up, just like that, in a moment. So, I move on to the next "thing" on my list. Jeff (my solicitor) wanted me to demand more things and more money as a divorce settlement. But suddenly all I want is freedom. To discover who I am. To be away from people who think they already know me.

As I load the last of my things into the old family four by four, I am overwhelmed by nostalgia. Perhaps it's the familiarity of packing a car on this drive. Perhaps it's leaving the house where two of our three children were born. Perhaps it's the memories of so much love and laughter. The pain hits me hard, not "our" house, just Tom's. He moves back this afternoon. The injustice almost robs me of my newfound determination. "One thing at a time," I say to myself. Get into the car, turn on the GPS, and follow the instructions.

The journey takes four days, two of which are on the ferry. I stay in a hotel in Ribadeo on the coast just inside Galicia. I feel strange in a hotel room on my own, but I want some thinking time. I want to arrive looking calm, prepared, and in control. I no longer feel like me; I have never driven this far, done anything like this by myself. I have never been just Jo, made decisions that affect me and no one else. My emotions swing between loneliness and liberation. I turn to point something out to Tom, but then remember he's not here. I wonder how long it will take for me to stop doing that.

The motorway is almost empty and takes me past forests first of pine and eucalyptus then the native chestnut and oak. I am headed inland into the heart of Galicia, to a village too small for the map. Only nine houses, three of which I will be responsible for. Of the others, one is a ruin, three are occupied. Two are holiday homes. I have learned the information sheet almost by heart I have read it so often.

I leave the motorway, driving on narrow country roads winding through the trees, and I am nervous. The trees clear as I reach the lane leading into the village, and I gasp. The village lies just below me—and beyond that miles of fields, trees, and mountains. There is a glint of water in the valley, and maybe a distant road. I stop the car, drinking in the view. Buzzards hang in the air and circle lazily in the sunshine, and I smile. I open the car window and notice how different the air smells, how clean. It is impossible not to smile. For the first time in quite a while, I see the future and it looks good.

I am to collect the keys from Maria at Number 4. She will show me the *casita* where I am to live. She speaks little English, so tomorrow one of the trustees, a local lawyer, also called Maria, will show me around. She will explain my responsibilities, and I will sign the final papers. She will help me with a bank account and the paperwork I need to live here. I park the car and walk around the village. The road is narrow and the houses are set in a circle around a tiny church and an even tinier graveyard. The weathered, grey-granite houses have mossy slate roofs. The slates are different sizes and set like fish scales. Each house is in a different position on the hillside at a different angle. Some have porches, some balconies, and one has a tiny patio with a bench. Roses grow up the walls and vines are trained over the lane.

Number 4 is long and low, with pots of flowers in rows along the length. I ring the bell and hear a cheerful voice shouting "*Un momento.*" I wait for ages, going over Spanish phrases in my head. Eventually, the door opens and a woman aged about forty peers out. "*Sí?*"

"*Soy Jo.*"

"*Sí*, The English. Welcome, welcome. Come, I have keys in *la Cocina.*" She chats away, freely mixing English and Spanish, and I feel more relaxed. Then she leads me along a passage beside the church to a tiny cottage I hadn't noticed earlier. The door opens directly into a kitchen. It is a charming mix of modern and old-fashioned. Maria is still talking. "There is food here and in the *refidgaredor*, but you must *comprar mas*. I will show you the *dormitorio.*" She opens a door I had not noticed. There is a staircase behind it leading to a huge landing, with a bed on one wall and a door at either end. One leads to a bathroom, the other to a bedroom filled with light and looking over the roofs of the village towards the view, which is so captivating. Maria continues, "There is a pantry and a storeroom for tools, but why not look later? Now you are tired and need a rest. Where is your suitcase?"

She is right. I am exhausted. She comes with me to the car and helps with my bags, and as the door closes behind her, I am indescribably lonely. There is no chance to be sad for long, though. The next few days are a blur. I talk to Maria, the lawyer, and Pedro, one of the trustees. I open a bank account, fill in paperwork, sign contracts, and eat meals with people I don't think I've ever met. I sleep because I am too tired at night to do anything else.

Today is Sunday. I've been here for a week and today is my first free day. No meetings or appointments. Maria, at Number 4, has invited me for lunch, but I decline. I have not yet unpacked my bags. There has been so much to do and see. She laughs, saying that I must never be lonely. I can come next week when her in-laws will also be there. It is amazing to have such neighbours. If only I can learn to speak enough Spanish to talk to them without help.

My little home is not a house but part of an outbuilding, turned years ago into a housekeeper's cottage and updated for my arrival. It has two wood stoves: the one in the kitchen is also a cooker and a water heater. There is another on the landing. I am glad that spring is turning into summer so I can delay learning how to use them. The kitchen is large and has a table, four chairs, a sofa, an armchair, and a television. There are big French doors leading to a sunny patch of grass behind the church. The grass is not mine, but a bench and a table are there for me to use.

The car is in the open barn next door. The pantry and the tool shed are through a door at the bottom of the stairs. They have filled the tool shed with a range of tools old and new for me to use. I am more than a little daunted, having no idea of their purpose. The big landing now has a desk and a chair. I've pushed the bed back against the far wall and someone is coming to install a telephone and Internet next week. I will need to keep in contact with the trustees, and soon I will be responsible for some of the paperwork as part of my job, so it will work well as an office. My clothes are hanging in the huge bedroom wardrobe, with the boxes I haven't unpacked alongside. I consider unpacking them now, but I decide instead to explore the houses and land for which I am responsible, or some of it at least.

The trustees gave me a whirlwind tour of the houses and a map of the land attached to each. The houses are huge. And despite land sales over the years, there is still well over two hundred hectares. They rent some out to neighbouring farmers and most is woodland. To my relief, I am not expected to become a farmer. They gave me a list of my duties, thankfully translated into English by Maria, the lawyer, but I haven't yet studied them. I still feel overwhelmed. I don't officially start until June, two weeks away, although my Spanish lessons start next week.

The first house is the smallest, but not small, and is empty apart from the old dining room on the first floor, which has been converted into a classroom. I am to teach English as part of my job, armed with my new Celta qualification. The academy is running and has a full-time teacher, Chelo, who also teaches maths and science. One bedroom is being furnished as a second classroom, and I will take over the two existing English classes and help to expand the academy.

The second house really is empty, cold, and unloved. It is solid and dry inside, with a courtyard with numerous outbuildings covered in vegetation. It is the third house that is the most interesting. It is huge. A "*palacio*," the equivalent of a stately home in Britain. They have covered all the furniture and paintings that remain inside in dust sheets. It lends an eerie atmosphere and there is room after room after room. Grand rooms, servants' quarters, vast kitchens, and the overgrown remains of what must have been beautiful landscaped gardens. Looking after the big house will take up most of my time. The trust doesn't have the money for a restoration, so I am part of the plan to halt the decline. I am to do a weekly rotation of inspection, noting anything that needs immediate attention and ensuring there is no access for vandals or thieves. I will also start on the gardens, clearing paths bit by bit until we can tell what's there. I will be a "drop in the ocean," a "doing something is better than nothing" kind of operation. The task strikes me as enormous beyond belief, and I take a deep breath, wondering how naïve the trustees must be to think I can make a difference here.

The third part of my job is to work with the trustees on some ideas for generating income for future restoration work. There is a pot of capitol invested, which generates interest enough for some repair work, taxes, running costs, and so forth. The academy now makes a profit that pays for the costs of that house, Chelo's salary, and a part of mine. It's still growing, so the hope is that in the new school year it will cover all of my costs. It also keeps the house warm and in good repair. It is a small thing, but it has given the trustees hope.

I already have an idea that involves turning my casita into a holiday let and moving into the academy There are three unused bedrooms and a functioning, if basic, kitchen there. I am so new here, though, that I don't want to rush in with ideas until I really understand my job, and besides which, I have grown to love the casita. I decide I will start a project book and add things through the winter when I have time for research. For now, I will concentrate on learning my job and getting to know the people I am to work with.

As the day-to-day routine of village life sets in, I find myself more and more curious as to why I am here. I mean, I know why I accepted the job and why I came. Remembering the day I came reminds me of the home that is no longer mine, it still upsets me, though my mind is clearer now. Surely no one is bequeathed a job in a will. I had been far too upset to question things as much as I should have. It had proved to be a way out, a solution to an immediate problem. I had been so devastated by what was happening to me, so afraid that my world was gone, that people were laughing at my stupidity. I took the chance to get away as a gift and without question.

With that thought and a mystery to solve, I realise that I have officially started my job with a heart that is much less burdened than when I arrived. Working in the fresh air in the most beautiful house and gardens I have ever seen in the most amazing setting I can imagine will be fantastic. Even my nervousness at my lack of qualification for the job hasn't intruded on the pure joy at the opportunities before me.

My questions about why the trustees offered me this job have so far got me nowhere. I keep being told that the job is mine for a year, at the end of which, if the trustees are happy with me and I with the job, they will invite me to a meeting to discuss the future of the project. If things go badly or I am unhappy, I will be free to leave at the end of my year's contract. It is an experiment of sorts. There is nothing else to say. I am told this every time I ask no matter how subtle I think I am being. If I stay on, they will give me more details. I am forced to accept that and go back to my resolution of taking one day and one thing at a time.

As spring days lengthen into long summer days, I develop a routine. On Wednesdays I have my Spanish lesson in town. I do my shopping. I meet one of the Marias in the afternoon. It is my people day, my business day. The other days I divide between path clearing in the morning; paperwork and projects over lunch, when it's really hot outside; and house inspections and vegetable gardening in the evening. I revel in the freedom. My teaching duties will start in October and will take my Tuesdays and

Thursdays, but for the moment I can take life at a steady pace. My social life is and will be for a while limited by my language skills. I work steadily, concentrating on the job at hand, and at night I am tired. My grief and betrayal, which I still feel, is contained now. If I am overwhelmed, I walk in the woods where there is no one to see my tears and let the beauty and tranquillity of my new home sooth my soul.

Winter takes me by surprise, arriving suddenly with rain like I have never seen. There is water everywhere. My house inspections are now about finding leaks in roofs. I buy Wellington boots and a waterproof coat. Umbrellas wait by the door. I grapple with the art of fire lighting. The fires become my lifeline and my comfort. The casita is transformed with a fire and barely liveable without. My work on the garden paths and the vegetable patch almost stops. Instead, I fill my time with teaching. My classes have overflowed into two extra hours. Chelo is thrilled and talks about the need for another teacher and more rooms. I tell her about my idea to let out the casita. We walk around the building and make plans. The two bedrooms overlooking the village would make a tiny apartment with the addition of a bathroom. I could share the kitchen with the school who will also use the room for the needed teachers' lounge. The big front bedroom would make another classroom and a tiny office. I would use the inside stairs. The children would use the balcony stairs, giving me at least the illusion of privacy. She is enthusiastic as are the trustees. We will spend the whole years' repair and restoration budget on the changes and work will begin in the spring.

Short days and long evenings are affecting my mood. I am lonely and missing the children, who called often when I first came, but have gone strangely silent. I haven't heard from Jeff about the last, trailing issues from the divorce settlement; he is a world and a lifetime away. I realise that I must take control of my past and my present. As I consider calling Jeff, I realise something that I should have realised much earlier. He was the one who told me about this job, so he must have more information. Why didn't I speak to him sooner? I think back to the initial conversation. It was Jeff who told me it was a bequest; What else does he know?

Maybe he knows how the children are and might nudge them into calling me. I have tried calling them to no avail.

"Oh, Hi, Jo." Jeff's response sounds reluctant and silence follows his greeting. Am I being paranoid? I'm not sure but he really doesn't sound happy to talk to me.

"Did something go wrong with the final divorce settlement? Were you unable to get the things I asked for? . . . I thought we had agreed on everything! . . . After all I really didn't want very much more than my share of the house. . . . But don't worry because I really have everything that I need already and . . ."

"Whoh," interrupted Jeff, sounding less serious. "Everything you wanted is in a small storage unit and you obviously haven't checked your savings account, because the money has already been transferred—more than you were expecting because I insisted on a full, independent valuation of house and contents. I know you thought it unnecessary, but, as it turns out it. made a huge difference. Actually, Jo, that's the good news, I don't really know how to tell you the rest, but Tom has taken advantage of your absence and told everyone that you broke up the marriage by having an affair that started years ago. I'm so sorry, but that's what he has told the children, both families and your friends."

Now it is my turn to be silent, I am so shocked. "Who with?" I squeak. Do people believe him? How could he?

Jeff's voice became guarded again. "Tom was angry with me for getting the valuation agreed by the court. He was sure he had everything his way. His lawyer had told him not to worry because I am incompetent, and they had bullied you into agreeing with anything. They both assumed that we would agree to their valuation. I guess people don't know what to believe about the affair and you're not here, which seems to make Tom's story more credible. I am sorry, I feel responsible."

"Don't be silly," I say briskly. "Who am I supposed to have had this affair with?"

"That's the worst part," was the sheepish reply. "With me, and at the moment you're supposed to be living in my holiday villa in Spain, sitting by the pool waiting for me to come and join you."

"I will put the phone down now and ring you back in exactly ten minutes, when I've thought of something to say," I say to him.

It was the bit about the villa and the pool that snaps me into my new reality. Six months ago It would have devastated me. Now I know exactly what I need to do. I phone Jeff back to apologise, explaining that I did not understand how vindictive or manipulative Tom could be. I tell him how grateful I am that he, as a friend, handled the divorce. I e-mail all three children and include photos of my little casita taken in the rain. I tell them that the only pool I had was by the door when the wind blew the rain from the road. I remind them that Jeff has never really gotten over his wife's death from cancer several years ago, still wears his wedding ring, and keeps her photo on his desk. I suggest they check the facts carefully before they think badly of him. I invite them to come and see me as soon as they can get a flight, because I needed to talk to them about the future.

The funny thing is that as soon as I have written the e-mails, I knew my future was here in Galicia. I even love the rain. I want to stay here and garden and walk and take care of things. The children come, one at a time, and we talk. I say nothing bad about Tom. I don't need to. He had fallen into the trap of assuming that Galicia was like southern Spain and so painted a picture that could never be true.

The day of the annual trustees' meeting has arrived. I know they want me to stay, though I am still nervous. I so badly want a permanent contract. When I arrive, I am surprised to find an almost party atmosphere. I am also surprised that all of my neighbours are here. Then I spot Jeff! Someone bangs on the table and speaks. Maria translates just in case. I am told that they are formally requesting me to stay on and I have to say whether I will accept a contract. I embarrass myself by being far too enthusiastic about how much I want to stay. I sit down red faced and confused. But the Chairman reads what is obviously someone's will. The translation is complicated and legal sounding. But it sounds as though the job I am being offered is chairman of the trustees, together with something to do with the house and monies.

We have to go to the Notary to sign the documents but I am obviously still puzzled, everyone. Everyone else in the room seems to be bursting with excitement and bottles and glasses are appearing on the table. Jeff and Maria, the lawyer, take me to one side. I have inherited the estate. They explain the owner felt indebted to my grandfather, who had saved his and his brother's lives by smuggling them out of the country during the civil war. My grandfather had loved Galicia and the house. As my grandfather had died, the owner had wanted to ensure that I loved it too.

If I agree, a deal has been done with the tax office to reduce the inheritance tax. The main house must be open to the public and administered by a board of trustees; it must, over time, be maintained and restored. I can live in the house or not as I choose and will receive a stipend. The land and smaller houses are mine with no conditions. My shocked brain couldn't really grasp all this, but both Jeff and Maria assure me it is real, that the deal involving the tax is good, and that I should sign.

So, I do.

Silence

Vanesa de La Puente Blanco

Yesterday, when I woke up, I was still in a dream. It was very difficult to separate reality from unreality, because I couldn't understand the way something real could be better than dreaming. I know it sounds as if I were crazy. Perhaps I am, I don't know. Does anybody know?

Where am I? That was the first question I asked myself? No answer.

What kind of paradise is this? The second question. Same answer: nothing.

Silence was the only partner I had—just silence. I closed my eyes to have breath and I tried to understand once and again what was happening to me. Silence, nothing more.

I strongly opened my eyes trying to capture everything around me. I started spinning in an outburst of bewilderment and running everywhere without knowledge, nervously. I was lost.

I sat down on a big stone and I started crying. Why? Silence disappeared. I let out a sigh of relief after I realized I wasn't alone. I could see some people walking and taking photos near the place I was. They were tourists, no doubt about it, because they were following instructions from a guide they carried. I stood up quickly but I walked slowly to where they were. I greeted them warmly in order to investigate about that place, telling them I had become disoriented while strolling in the field. One of them took out the canteen and she offered it to me. I drank a sip of water and I immediately felt better. I was pleased to meet them. I still didn´t know if I was dreaming or not, but I felt calm. It was great.

I joined the tourist group and we got down to a jetty in the Sil River. There was a boat and my new travel mates invited me to get on board with them. It sounded funny, so I did it. The river became wider and wider. It had millions of liters of water running quickly following the same way as if they knew perfectly where to go, not like me. The curvature of the meander could be appreciated while sailing. It was an incredible experience. I looked around myself once and again thinking about what I was supposed to do or to say staying with those people I didn't know. I was happy, that's a fact, but I felt a little bit embarrassed for being in front of strangers who probably thought I was mad.

Vineyards, forests, stones, water. Nothing else was necessary in that marvelous place. At that moment I knew it wasn't a dream because I could feel the cold air caressing my face.

The tourist guide on the boat explained to us that the place we were in was A Ribeira Sacra, in Galicia. Instantly, I remembered that I had chosen Ourense and Lugo to spend my holidays, so that was the reason for being there: I was on holiday. That explained my clothes too, because I was wearing shorts and a T-shirt, something unusual for me.

I was amazed about the explanations of my new teacher. The guide told us how people in those lands still worked like their ancestors did, because of the characteristics of the place. They loved and respected their popular traditions. It was lovely. To advance doesn't mean to change customs. Progress doesn't suppose the destruction of the origin.

I spent the day with my new friends, visiting wine cellars, monasteries, paths, and great restaurants. It was the best experience I have ever had. It was the first time in my life that I was spontaneous. I liked it.

* * * *

At night I understood what had happened to me. After being ten years working in a city, I decided to go on holiday to A Ribeira Sacra in order to relax. I think my body felt exhausted when I had clean air in my lungs and my mind couldn't process that new information: NATURE.

I felt it had been a good decision.

I woke up. Silence. Good morning. Very good morning.

My name is not an important detail now. I am a writer who rarely sells her books, because "they are not good enough". That´s what my editor says. I know I´ll write one best-seller in my life, at least. When? No idea. Till that time, I am trying to live situations that add experience to me, in order to enrich my texts. That´s the reason for being here now.

My grandmother was born in a small town called Alais in A Ribeira Sacra, but she had to move when the Civil War finished. I hate what I have read about that horrible period. I don´t like what my Grandma told me about the situations she had to live. She lived thirty years more or less in Vitoria, a small city in Spain. Being a woman was difficult.

For women, living in the Twenty-first Century is easier than living in the Renaissance. For women, living in the Renaissance was easier than in The East Meadow. In Roman times, human sacrifices were made. There is a song in Spain that says *"cualquier tiempo pasado nos parece mejor"*, which means that every past time seems to be better, but it's a fake. The passing of time makes everyone age, of course, and learn about made mistakes. Women are the engine of this society like the heart is the motor organ of the body. We have the key to open people's future, but for that, we have to open our minds first. I am here in this moment because I want to fight to get the world I want to stay in. That's our task, our sense of duty.

What don't I want?

I want no plastic in our oceans, I want no violence in our homes, I want no global heating, I want no sexism . . . A lot of changes are needed. Let's start making things.

I want to wake up every day being the woman I am. That's the way I feel today: I am the woman I want to be in the world I want to live in.

Remember this name, María López Quintela, my Grandma's name.

For her. For me. For us.

This travel to A Ribeira Sacra is the starting line at the beginning of my new life. I needed say good-bye to my Grandma in her motherland because she died last year in Vitoria and I felt that it couldn't be our last farewell. She thought that when people die their souls go up to Heaven. I don´t share that thought, but I needed to make peace with her doing what she desired: coming here and letting her go. I needed to make what she desired.

Yesterday, I was a woman who had to clean her soul. Today, I am at peace with myself.

This is the first time I visit A Ribeira Sacra, but I can certainly say that it will not be the last, because now I am in love with these lands. I can breathe not only air but life.

My name does not still matter. I am a writer. I´ll write my own story.

Yesterday, when I woke up, I was still in a dream. My Grandma was next to me.

She looked at me fixedly.

What will become of me, Grandma? I asked.

Silence. Sometimes, having no answer is the best answer.

I am the answer.

One Year in Galicia

Sarah Newton Jones

Music and sacred river wine,
The surprise of others in quiet
Public places no longer surprising but of interest;
This shared green canvas—for it is truly shared—
Together, a mix of sturdy natives and western elopers,
No longer running the solo races of an
Urban network where we were antlike—
frenetic, sound bites and power lines,
In comparison to this Galicia, where we are all
Fleshed out, with time to settle three-dimensional,
And known by our words
In the still air,
And in silhouette among the trees.
A wink in a cafe studs a tale of growing familiarity—
Life is fresh and raw and the convent bells ring just on our clocks
And we are gently concerned with
Making a living,
By hand,
And giving time to love loved ones
To learning love in the simpler moments.

The Dog with No name

Heath Savage

Weeks after moving into our house in Panton we began to become familiar with the faces of villagers. We did not know them and had not yet met them, so we named them ourselves, or learned their nicknames, from the men who were renovating our house. Fond recognition of these characters helped us to begin to feel at home. "Phil Oakey", "Homer Simpson", and "Il Postino" would stop and say *ola* as they sauntered around, at a pace that would place them in danger of being trampled in Sydney. We had names allocated to us too: "Las damas Australianas".

The day after we moved in, our neighbour's dogs introduced themselves. One barged into the kitchen, rolled onto her back, and demanded the attention that the previous owners of our home had taught her to expect. She had also learned from them that leaving without a snack was not an option. Her shy, doddery companion hung back, unsure of us. Unsteady, nearly blind, and completely deaf, she navigated life behind her bolder, smarter pal. She had fluffy, white fur, so we called her Snowy, and her friend with the mismatched eyes, Maria.

We got to know other dogs too, as we walked our international jet-setting Chihuahua-cross, Raphael. We sat in the village square drinking coffee with him beside us—something we were never permitted to do in rule-raddled Sydney. A sweet-natured giantess came and introduced herself, sniffed Raphael, then abandoned him for my churro. She was Nesca. A squishy-faced little bruiser with bags of attitude and a remarkable under-bite was Pauwel. A flirtatious little Maltese lady, who made eyes at Raphael, then lavished him with delicate kisses, was Fortunata.

One odd-bod little fellow with silken black and white fur and spaniel ears trotted behind them all on short, muscular legs that turned up into huge paws. His luxurious tail was a feathery flag that he waved all the time. He followed everyone human too, seeking friendly attention, but he was more often ignored. Some people fed him table scraps, which he ate delicately and slowly, unsure of when more might come.

We would see him lie at one particular spot on the fringe of the village, head on paws, waiting. Day after day. Week after week. A new friend told us that he followed her and her two dogs, Merlin and Maggie, on their daily walks. He followed our neighbour too, through the woods with his Labrador, Rodney. He called him "Shadow". We named him "Stumpy".

Stumpy began to appear with "Snowy and Maria", whom we now knew by their real names, Pinta and Karolina, every day. He would follow them down the lane and lie forlornly under the balcony of a ruin behind our house, out of the rain, shuddering with cold and wet through. Raphael would wag his tail at him through the sitting room window and then retire to his soft bed and fleece blanket. The spoiled rich kid.

We started to feed Stumpy each time we saw him. And he never refused. Patting him, we could feel his ribs under the long fur, and closer inspection revealed many fleas and ticks, which we rid him of as best we could. So, we started to groom him properly and gave him a Seresto collar. We laid some cardboard and an old blanket down on the spot where he lay. He began to run to welcome us when we opened our gate and enjoyed the fussing and affection we lavished on him. After many weeks he began to return each night to sleep on the blanket.

As autumn turned and the cold grew sharper, Stumpy's fur would be stiff with frost; he would shiver as he devoured his breakfast. We added warm water and vitamins or a raw egg to the mix. He would delicately pick out all the biscuits first, then lap the meaty gravy, but not before a thorough patting and loving had been enjoyed! A friend donated a plastic dog bed; we bought him a waterproof mattress and layered more blankets on. Stumpy revelled in the new luxury and would spend the colder days lying on his back, snoring.

We wondered if his owners missed him, so we made enquiries. Then our electrician confirmed it—he knew him and knew where he had lived with his family; Stumpy was *abandonado*. He and his brother, who had vanished a year before, had been simply left behind when the family moved away. The empty house was where Stumpy lay each day awaiting their return, before coming to his new bed and the strange Australian ladies who had fallen in love with him.

We called out our vet, and Stumpy stepped into the van, fearful of the smells, but sweet and gentle. A thorough examination revealed that he was intact, about three years old, and in very good health. He was vaccinated, wormed, and given tick protection. A new, smart collar went on beside the Seresto, and Stumpy became Mario.

Mario comes when he is called, enjoys treats and regular meals, but is a free spirit, wary of confined spaces and indoors. He still sleeps in the old alpendre while we finish our house. Snoozing at our back door most days, sheltering from the newly bright sunshine, he flings himself at our feet for belly rubs as we pass back and forth. He is still one of the Three Amigos, trotting around the village on those huge feet behind Pinta and Karolina. Mario returns each day to claim his spot at the door of his new home with his new family, who will never abandon him.

Ferreira Wildlife—First Impressions—

Sarah Newton Jones

A stork stands tall then rises to the air,
Bearing twigs for her unruly nest
Perched on the roof of an oblong municipal building—
Visible for miles,
Wing sweeps audible in the still crisp day.
Three neighbourhood dogs linger at our gate,
Rolling on their backs for a rub of bellies, they are now
Visiting daily
We participate with treats and discuss them with affection.
Our own small Australian dog
Nuzzles them through the gate and calmly wags.
Flash on the road and from our wall—a snake—
Frightened we
Call in our dog.
Alerted we are.
Dragonflies mate in mid-air on a pond made by friends,
Bees inspect our clothing then settle on a bloom.
Out of the corner of an eye a cat slinks around the path.
Our own small Australian cat stays inside, safe, warm,
Her belly content and thick in her thirteenth year,
Her first here in Galicia.

Winter, What Is It Like?

Stephen Bush

In Australia what winter is like varies; in Spain it varies even more. I made the change and now I could have a day of snow in winter, something not possible in any of the places I lived in Australia. But in summer in Galicia, in the Ribeira Sacra, it will be in the 30s, or should I say, in Fahrenheit, from the mid 80s to the mid 90s, with cool nights. In Australia it tended to stay hot at night if it was a hot day, but not here.

Winter starts in earnest in late October in Galicia. The days can still be warm enough for swimming in the Minho River during the first week or two of October, but by now the fires will be lit at night to keep the house warm. It is past the time to make sure you have a good supply of wood and to make sure there is enough gasoil in the tank if you have central heating running on that.

If you are an organized person with land with trees growing on it, preferably Spanish oak trees, they burn the hottest and longest, you will have cut your wood and brought it home and put in the barn in May or even April. You will have time in those months for woodcutting and carting and stacking before you need to start working on your grapevines and on your huerta, your vegetable garden.

The Ribeira Sacra is a place of definite seasons, unlike most of Australia, where they tend to gradually arrive, and definitely not like Northern Australia, where it is always hot and the only variation is if it is raining daily or not raining at all—the Wet Season and the Dry Season, as they are known. There are no such things as autumn and spring there.

The native pine forests on the steep river banks of the Sil and Minho rivers in the Ribeira Sacra are green all year, but the Spanish oaks and most other trees shed their leaves in autumn in a brief display of restrained color. The occasional patches of American oaks are an exception, their dying leaves being bright red. The Spanish oaks are far more bland. The grasses die off and things are quiet on the huerta, with the last produce picked by late October or occasionally early November. I have picked the last green tomatoes that late. Down in the river valleys of the Minho and Sil things grow for longer than they do higher up where it is cooler and windier.

Winter arrives gently and is coldest in late January and in February, but when we had a big snowfall here a couple of years ago it was in March. Winter likes to jump up and surprise you just when you think it is starting to leave. The snow started falling in the very early hours and fell on into the morning. It didn't sit for long, though. It was over a foot deep on the ground when it stopped falling and had mostly disappeared within twenty-four hours. Apparently, thirty or forty years ago there was a big snowfall in the village and people were trapped here for a week, but that was before everyone had a car and the road was worse.

The snow fell too early to affect the grapes. But that year was also a wet year and that did affect them. The grapes grown in the thousands of small terraced vineyards rising up from the rivers Minho and Sil, the home of what is proudly called "Heroic" viticulture, are the most important thing in the lives of many people in the Ribeira Sacra. Ribeira Sacra means Sacred Riverbank and the name comes from the middle ages when there were numerous monasteries along the river.

Years before the monasteries the Romans lived here and mined gold and made wine. This is a rich region. The Minho and the Sil rivers join together at Os Peares, and the Minho continues to the Atlantic and, on the last part of its journey, provides the border between Portugal and Spain. There it runs between the wonderfully preserved heavily fortified towns of Tui on the Spanish side and Valenca on the Portuguese side.

Os Peares is now the home of one of the many small-to-medium-sized hydroelectric dams built by Spanish dictator Francisco Franco along these two rivers. Before the dams were built in the 1960s there was no bitumen road linking the villages along the Minho, only a dirt one dating from ancient times, and the rivers provided the transport to take the wine to the bigger cities along the riverbanks. The rivers were also full of salmon and trout, now long gone and replaced by black bass, a destructive fish from the United States.

In summer the roads in the Ribeira Sacra are almost bustling with tourists and people tending their vineyards, building to a crescendo of tourists in August and then in late September or early October to a plethora of vineyard workers here for the grape harvest, Vendimia. Now roads that are usually deserted see large trucks arrive to take away the grapes picked by hand on numerous small vineyards and carried up to the road in cubos, plastic containers, by hardy locals, many in their sixties and seventies, the "Heroic" viticulture. On the Sil there are vineyards where the grapes go on boats to the bodegas, as there is no other way to get to the grapes.

But in winter the Ribeira Sacra is left to the people living here who can enjoy having empty roads again, taking holidays while there is no work to do, or just relaxing by the "economo" in the kitchen. This cast-iron wood-fired cooking stove, built with bricks and cast-iron pieces, is still found in most village kitchens, including mine, and was often formerly built in the center of the room, like an island, with a wooden bench along the back of it to sit on to keep warm. The parts are still made in Spain and can be bought new for installation in your kitchen. Or maybe they sit by one of the modern versions of a wood-cooking stove used for central heating, like a friend of mine has.

It is not so many years ago that winter meant sitting almost on top of the small cooking fire burning on a stone hearth at one side of the small room used for preparing food. These can still be seen in many old houses. It was a much colder life back then unless you had a good number of cows or sheep living in the barn under your floor that were providing lots of extra heat to your house.

The best things about winter here are the peace and quiet of having few people about; the clean air, which is so pure that even going to the local village can seem like going into a cloud of noxious pollution; the magical views; and the wildlife.
There is definitely a lot of good to a winter life in the Ribeira Sacra region of Galicia.

The Final Choice

Adrian Chiclana Casanova

There is only one Greenland
although,
there are a lot of green lands
in this world.
Are you looking to visit them all?
You will have to walk, walk!
Not a bit, a lot!
What would be one reason for walking?
To feel stronger, the touches of life,
inside our chest.
The heart of the dead does not beat.
We live in one green land,
but this green
made of thousands of greens,
loves all colours.
Whether they replace it
from the leaves
through the seasons,
or accompany it
in the luminous traces
of the rose windows
of middle ages.
Galicia is the land
of the thousand rivers.
Each one of them,
with its own voice.
From soprano to bass.
Beautiful choir land.
Among water arteries,
we are between
two of them.
The Miño and Sil rivers,

for us, two deep kisses.

But relationships are not always good,
and humans can be locusts.
Maybe it was written in our DNA,
in some lost locus.
In the actual world,
some rivers forgot
that they once,
were crystalline . . .

What is our final choice, **Still Life or Living Nature?**

==================Loading answer.....................

Amalie

{Amalie is a novel in progress aimed at middle grade children.}
                                                              JP Vincent
(Second Place winner Prose Fiction 2019)

Chapter 1

> *La Voz 25th May 2019*
> *Sepultura de Vilacha*
> *Whilst excavating in the Vilacha area, archaeologists have discovered a Bronze Age skeleton in a sepulture. Overlooking the Sil, Os Conventos is where the team have uncovered many remains of the era. The team believe this area was the frontier between different clans, and the finds placed deliberately for symbolic reasons. The symbols are typical of the Atlantic cultures and articles found in Britain. They are from the middle-to-late Bronze Age. The individual burials found were only for soldiers who died in battle or high-ranking officials. A female skeleton, they believe was the head of a clan, was also found near the entrance of this ancient castro.*

> *It would have pleased Amalie that the skeletons of her parents survived for three thousand years. That they will be part of a new story, recognition of their lives.*

> *However, this story is Amalie's:*

$$* * * *$$

Amalie stood at the edge of the escarpment and looked down along the river Sil. She could see the long, dugout boats, fully laden with goods, working their way down the river to the sea. She could see the oarsmen pulling in unison on their long, wooden oars—a hard row even with the current in their favour.

The wind whipped her long, dark hair across her tear-stained face, a curl caught in her wooden ear stud. A spring day, and the sun warmed her long, bare arms and legs. Her pale woollen tunic, woven by her mother, lay soft on her skin. Her plaited skirt, crafted by both her mother and her during the long winter, felt fresh and new.

Half a moon ago, a sick stranger came to their *castro* (village) of Os Conventos. Amalie's mother took pity on him and nursed him in their roundhouse. Her mother, as head of their small clan, warranted the largest building, but it also doubled as a meetinghouse and a centre for anyone sick or injured. Her mother, knowledgeable with herbs and incantations, was the person anyone went to for cures, medicines, and advice. She was a kind, gentle woman who never turned anyone away. However, she couldn't cure this stranger, no matter which herbs she gave him or incantations she spoke, or offerings to the gods. He died. Within a week, the stranger's fever took her mother, father, and young brother. Amalie buried them, in their stone tombs, the following day, as was their custom. She placed their tools, some food, and their favourite objects alongside them for their journey into the afterlife. Her brother, for his comfort, she placed alongside her mother. He wasn't a grown man and did not warrant his own tomb.

For fear of catching the sickness, the rest of the clan stayed away from the funeral. Amalie chanted the words to send them off on their journey into the afterlife, as her mother would have. She added her own personal messages to the family she lost, through her mother's goodness. She was content she'd sent them into their next life fully equipped.

She was keen to begin her own journey.

* * * *

Her pony, a hardy mountain breed, short and sure-footed, waited for her at the entrance of the castro. She had already strapped her panniers onto his back and he was ready to leave.

She watched the boats leave the little wooden jetty, below their castro. They contained her father's bronze axe heads, knives, and arrowheads. The boats were headed toward the spring gathering and market in Los Pericos on the coast.

She walked down from the escarpment toward her pony. He whickered in greeting.

82

Her father spent his life creating beautiful objects from the precious metals, copper and tin. He not only made weapons, but also fine pieces of jewellery for her mother and her. She stroked the armlet on her forearm, with its intricate patterns, the style a secret message between her father and her. Packed into the boat with her father's pieces were precious herbs, picked the previous summer by her mother and dried for remedies, salves, potions, and recipes. She would need these for her new life wherever her journey led her. Either to sell or for her own use.

The boatmen refused to take her, their fear of the sickness overcoming their need for a fee-paying passenger and the long boats were too small to carry a stocky pony. Her journey would be different from the boats, because she didn't want to leave her faithful pony and let him return to the wild. The boatmen's refusal meant she could make her own journey with her friend and constant companion, Roble, the pony. Her journey would take her through many small castros, larger towns, down through canyons and up over the mountains to the coast. She would meet the boats, which carried all her trading goods, at Os Pericos, where the goods would be sold at the market. This had been the family's plan before tragedy struck. Also, the original plan included meeting Amalie's mate. At fourteen she was old enough to start her own family. Amalie trusted her father would choose a good man for her, but she was nervous about meeting her suitor. The only information she had about him was his name, that he had a trade, and his family origins.

She checked the panniers on the back of Roble, the sheepskin pad held on by straps. Two large bags contained all her tools and goods for her journey: her mother's soft woollen cape, amber and shale beads for currency, a small fishing net, and as much food from the roundhouse as she could carry. She patted Roble and leapt onto his back. She could feel the other members of the clan watching behind the rough curtains hanging in their doorways. She sighed. Before the sick stranger arrived, she had friends, family, and a wonderful carefree life. Now her friends avoided her and her family members were dead. Every decision from now on would be hers and hers alone. She felt unequal to the task ahead of her.

Chapter 2

Lemavos

The Sun was at its height when they finally left. Amalie decided to make for Lemavos (Monforte de Lemos), a hill castro. She knew they could make it by nightfall and stay with her relatives in the area. The name Lemavos means green and fertile valley. Her relations were skilled farmers. Roble, pleased to be moving, set off at a jog. They followed the ridges of the hills, above the tree line, where it was easier to walk. After a while, the countryside sloped down toward Lemavos and the verdant green plain.

Although the ground was boggy, the pony found it softer underfoot than the rough tracks they'd ridden along up on the ridges. As the sun disappeared over the horizon, they reached her aunt's hovel in the lee of the hill. The smells from the open door caused her stomach to grumble. She was famished, not a morsel of food having crossed her lips during her time of mourning. She leapt off her pony, took off the heavy panniers, and hobbled Roble so he could go and find food but not go off too far. She took the panniers into the house, and a barrage of warm greetings met her. There were hugs and tears and chaos as each of the family members wanted her story.

"Amalie, you look so thin." her aunt said, dishing up a pottery bowl of thick broth. "Come in and sit down. Move over and let your cousin sit," She admonished a young boy, who looked up at Amalie with awe. She presented a vision of cascading hair, long limbs, and confidence. Her bronze armlet glinted in the glow of the cooking fire, adding to the illusion.

Amalie smiled at the boy. She was hungry and tired after their journey and the day's events. She sat beside him, the fire and the broth warmed her, and she was glad to be among family.

"You are so kind, Aunty. It has been a terrible time for me and it's good to be amongst family," Amalie said. The sadness she felt came through in her voice. "I have a long journey ahead of me to reach the coast and the annual market," she continued.

"Why do you have to go? You could stay here, if you wanted," her aunt asked. "We can find you a place and help you find a mate," she continued.

Amalie shook her head. "No thank you, Aunt. My father found me a mate and I'm to meet him at the gathering." She continued eating. The hot broth warmed her, tiredness overtook her, and her aunt led her to the sheepskin-covered straw bed at the edge of the house.

"Go and check Amalie's pony," she called out to her son as he edged out of the door in the hope of avoiding any chores.

She woke the following morning to the smell of a cooked breakfast. She yawned and stretched. Nothing had disturbed her during the night. "Morning," she said to her aunt. The flatbreads her aunt was cooking on the hot stones in the central fire created a delicious aroma. "They smell wonderful," she added and rose to get a closer look at the food.

"The men and boys have already left for the fields. It's sowing time," her aunt said. "Do you want to wash?"

Amalie pulled at her unruly hair and said, "Yes, please."

"There's a pitcher of water out the back and some twigs for your teeth."

"Thanks." Amalie went and washed. She brushed out the tangles in her hair with the bone comb, which belonged to her mother. She cleaned her teeth with the twigs and went back into her aunt's house. Her aunt hollowed out the cooked bread to hold a porridge-type meal and handed it to Amalie. "Thanks," Amalie said, as her aunt sat down beside her.

"What happened with the stranger? And why weren't you stricken with the fever?" Her aunt's bluntness surprised Amalie and she choked on the soft bread.

"I was away," she mumbled her mouth full of food.

"Where were you?"

"I was up in the hills with Roble. I'd gone hunting for rabbits and I had collected my catch, ready to go home, when my friends found me. We decided to camp out in the woods. We skinned, cleaned. and cooked the rabbits. Then we made frames to dry the pelts. We thought they would be good for hats and collars for the winter. After a couple of days drying, the pelts were ready to be taken down to the castro. We loaded them onto Roble's back and thought how pleased mum and dad would be. It was a fine haul. My friends and I knew nothing about the sickness or the deaths of the stranger and my family. Old Kuno, the cripple, stopped us at the entrance of the castro, he warned us not to come in as there was sickness. I didn't know it was in my house." She put her head in her hands as sadness hit her small frame and tears welled and spilled onto the rough wooden table.

"You were a very lucky girl." Her aunt patted Amalie's shoulder. "But why are you walking to the gathering? Why didn't you go by boat with your trades? Those boatmen will rob you!" her worried aunt asked.

"They wouldn't take me because of the sickness. I didn't want to leave Roble to the wilderness. He wouldn't know how to survive," Amalie said, finishing her breakfast. "I have to leave soon. Where's the best place to sleep tonight?"

"You'll be heading in the right direction if you keep the sun on your left shoulder. You will get further on that pony of yours than if you walked. Asma is a good place to stop." She pushed her hand up into the brush roof and pulled out a small, round object. "This token will give you safe passage and a place to stay." She handed the round, flat, bronze token to Amalie. "When you reach Asma ask for Edsel, the potter."

"Thank you, Auntie." She hugged the older woman, picked up her panniers, and left the hovel. Outside Roble saw her, whickered his greeting, carefully hobbled over, and waited for release. She bent down, untied his leather ties, and rubbed his legs "Sorry, Roble." She slung the panniers over his back and secured them. Her aunt came out carrying a flatbread, some cheese. and a few dried fruits wrapped in a rough cloth. Amalie packed the food into the pannier and thanked her aunt. She leapt up onto Roble and settled herself on the sheepskin pad. He was glad to be free from his ties, and he trotted off down the track toward the west.

Chapter 3

Asma

The journey along the green and verdant valley was a joy. The climb up to the first of many hill ranges was difficult, but they managed to wind their way through the underbrush. Their path twisted its way through the giant trees. The spring buds gave the canopy a light green hue. It was shady and she travelled keeping her shadow on her right. They reached the pinnacle and the view astounded her. In front of her was a sheer cliff down into the canyon of the Mino River. The sheer sides were criss-crossed by narrow shale tracks, made by the passage of the many mountain goats. She would have to lead Roble; it was far too dangerous to ride. They also had to cross this river, but where, she didn't know, and was too high up to recognise a good place to cross.

"'Okay, Roble, which way?" The cold wind blowing up through the canyon decided her. Keep the wind to her back. She thought the pony would always follow. But to be sure, she unpacked a plaited horsehair cord and tied it loosely around his neck. They began their descent. The shale rocks were slippery underfoot, and it was more of a scrabble and slide even on the widest parts. She understood now why most people and goods went by river. "Careful, Roble," she said when the pony's nose dug her in the back after he lost his footing. She grabbed a low branch to stop herself slipping when the ground gave way under her yet again. They reached the river when the sun was at its height. It blazed into the canyon, and Amalie began to sweat in her woollen top.

"We'll have our food here and then go for a swim," she said. Roble nuzzled her in reply. She unpacked the pony's bags, and he found a small area of sand to have a roll. He wandered off in search for fresh spring grass.

After eating her food, she clambered up onto an outcropping boulder and leapt into the water. She gasped when the freezing water took her breath away and laughed. She swam toward the pony and splashed him. He had walked down to drink at the edge of the water. "Coward, come on in." The pony eyed her whilst she swam in the deep, dark water. Her next task was to catch a couple of fish for her supper. She took the finely plaited net out of her pannier and dipped it into the running water. "Damn, they're too far out." She hunted for a long pole to attach to her net. Within a few minutes, she caught two fat. brown trout. "Perfect," she said and held them up for Roble to admire. He didn't look impressed.

She dressed and repacked the pony and they continued upstream, whilst looking for a crossing. The canyon narrowed as they headed further. Large boulders stuck out above the fast-flowing water. Could she cross here, she wondered. She could, but not Roble. A short distance on and she found a makeshift bridge. Stone slabs lay across the boulders to create a crude but sturdy crossing. She climbed up onto the first boulder. "Come on, Roble, it might be miles before we find another crossing," she said, and encouraged the pony to follow her. She walked to the other side and called him. He refused to move or jump up onto the boulder.

"Come on, Roble," she called again and again, and finally, with one huge leap, he plunged into the fast-flowing river. It was too fast for him and he got caught up in the current and was carried downstream. The now-soaked panniers didn't help and the weight made his struggle worse. He struck out with his hooves and thrashed the water, panic in his eyes, as the current took him. Amalie ran down the other side of the river calling and calling him to swim toward her. The thick undergrowth tangled around her feet and she fell to the ground, she despaired.

The river widened to allow the pony to find his feet and swim to shore. He shook off the water and stood, shaking with cold and fear at the water's edge. Amalie, scratched and bleeding from her fall, ran up and hugged him. She sobbed into his thick, wet coat. He didn't whicker this time. She pulled up some long grass, rubbed him down and took off the sodden panniers.

"Look at this mess," she said. The panniers contained all her possessions and they were sodden. She pulled out wet clothes, her mother's cape, and the not-so-dried skins and lay them over branches to dry. She lifted out and unwrapped her father's dies for making axe heads and knife blades. The lumps of grey metal and the blue copper stones, ready for mixing and firing, weren't damaged or lost. The amber and slate beads she needed for currency, taken from her mother's necklace, felt warm in her hand as she checked they were all there. She needed some currency before she could sell her father's work at the market. If, as her aunt said, the boatmen hadn't robbed her.

The boatmen and their loads would reach Os Pericos in seven days. She had plenty of time to get there before them.

The beads were beautiful, round, hard, and pearlescent. She took them out of the small rabbit skin bag and rolled them across the palm of her hand. Her mother wore them everyday threaded onto a long leather thong. The clasp was a tin button fashioned by her father. She lay her mother in her tomb with the necklace but only left a few beads. She held the remainder in her hand.

Her father's dies she would use to forge knives and small axe heads. This would be a long way into her unknown future. The large axe head die she lay with her father, in his tomb, for his journey into the afterlife. She could earn a living from forging. During the long cold winters her father taught her some of his forging skills. It was the warmest place to be—by the fire and with the man she most admired. She felt for the knife on her belt, her first knife, a short narrow blade for killing and skinning small animals. The wooden handle had a tin button and stamped with the family motif, a circle with a cross through it. She pulled it out of its sheath and rolled it over her hand. The knife was a thing of beauty, fitted into her hand and easy to use.

The sun dipped below the canyon wall. They weren't going to make Asma tonight. She gathered wood to make a fire. Without the warmth of the sun, the temperature dropped rapidly. Roble, recovered from his swim, dried out and was content to eat the fresh spring grass alongside the river. She would cook the two fish, for her supper that she'd caught earlier in the day.

Local Limericks

JP Vincent

Lugo

There was a young Roman called Hugo
Who was posted to far away Lugo.
His skirt was quite short
And his knees oft' got caught
By the wild and wicked wind around Lugo.

Monforte de Lemos

There once was a young man from Monforte.
Who was known to be fit and quite sporty.
He showed off his abs
To a young girl called Babs
That fit, flirty, young man from Monforte.

Growing up in Galicia

Andrea Jones

"When I get back from my holiday in the UK, I'm going to get a job and leave home," I announced out of the blue. Mum must have given a sigh of relief, although, to her credit, it was quite inaudible. "What holiday?" she asked. Mmmm . . . maybe I had forgotten to mention I had bought tickets to take my boyfriend to the UK to meet my family and see my hometown.

Mum and I didn't have an easy relationship. My parents had separated and subsequently divorced when I was a baby and I had lived with my grandparents until the age of six. I had had a very loving family background, and being the first grandchild, with my two uncles, both bachelors still living at home, I guess I may have been spoilt. I never hit it off with my stepfather, either. My first recollection of him was when he was the coalman who delivered the coal to my granddad and, in my eyes, he was the equivalent of the bogeyman. I don't exactly remember how it came about, but I was supposed to buy him an orange cap, which every week I failed to produce, so when I heard the coal lorry I would hide trembling under my bed. Imagine my dismay when my mum told me we were going to move in with him into another house away from my beloved grandparents.

However, things got even worse. A year later I was bundled into a motor caravan and taken away on a long trek around Europe until we finally settled in a tiny village near a small town called Monforte de Lemos. For a few months, we lived with a Spanish family in the village. My stepfather had close ties with them, as the oldest daughter had emigrated to the UK and had married an English chef, ending up as next-door neighbours to my stepfather during his first marriage. One of her sisters had been an au pair for his children and he had visited the family on numerous occasions prior to getting together with my mum. The Spanish family were lovely and a constant source of fascination for me, an only child, as they had eleven children. Some of them were grown up and married, with children of their own. A couple of the boys were away doing their military service. One sister was a nun, and the youngest was just three years older than I was. The house itself was fascinating, too. It was a bit like a rabbit warren, numerous rooms leading one into another so to get to bed you had to go through several other bedrooms. There was a beautiful bathroom, courtesy of the sister in England, which was the mum's pride and joy, but which was just a showpiece as it didn't actually have running water.

Finally, my mum and stepfather bought a piece of land, which at that time was just a gorse field at the foot of a small mountain, about a kilometre away from the nearest neighbours, and they set about clearing it to build a house. Once it was cleared, we went back to England and exchanged the motor caravan for an old car and a huge caravan, which was our home for the next few years as the house was slowly being built. They had also gone back to the UK in order to get married as at the time they were both divorced but hadn't married. Divorce was not legal in Spain at that time and not being married caused quite a lot of problems as my mum had no legal rights.

* * * *

Things didn't really improve much for the next few years. I rebelled by refusing to learn the language. There was no point; I didn't intend to live there long. Then one night after we had been visiting some friends of my stepfather's, who were of Galician origin but lived in the UK and whose children spoke both languages, I was dozing off on the backseat of the car when I heard him saying to my mother that it was a shame I was too stupid to learn Spanish. That was like a red rag to a bull, and the next day I decided I would speak Spanish. I guess that during the months I had spent there immersed in the language I had been picking it up, so by the time I started at the local village school I was fluent.

I never really integrated or made many friends. I had one best friend, but we lost touch with each other when we went to different high schools as she was from another village. I met my future husband when I was fifteen, through his cousin, who was my classmate during my first year at high school. It had been a very difficult year for me. Firstly, I had had my hopes raised when on the 23rd of February there had been an attempted military coup. My stepfather had come home early from work and we had started packing our basic necessities in case we had to leave suddenly. They followed the event on the BBC, what little information there was. However, the situation was defused and to my disappointment, we stayed.

Then during the summer holidays, I had told my mum I wanted to go to England to see my grandparents on a surprise visit. I had taken some of my savings out of the bank and bought my tickets, although my intention was to stay there. I now realise as a mum myself, I can't have been an easy teenager. I refused to let my mum contact my grandparents and I flew to Luton airport and made my own way to Wolverhampton. In those days, communication wasn't easy. We had no phone, nor did my grandparents. When I finally got there, I had to go to my uncle's house and phone the bar where my parents went most evenings and leave a message to say I had arrived safely.

However, my intention of moving back to the UK never materialised. I suddenly saw my grandparents with different eyes. They were getting older and it wasn't fair to ask them to take on a teenager, especially one so headstrong as myself. I contacted my dad to see if it was possible to live with him, but my stepmother had made it clear on my previous visit that I wasn't very welcome, and in any case there was no room for me as they lived with my seven step-siblings and half-siblings in a small house. So, I made the most of my holiday and went back, with the knowledge that I had to remain in Galicia for another three years at least, until I was eighteen. Therefore, when my boyfriend, my future husband, and I met, it was a very intense relationship in spite of our tender ages.

* * * *

I had always intended to leave home as soon as I was eighteen. But I was at a bit of a loss as what to do. I had wanted to go to university to be a nurse or a vet, but my stepfather was not only unwilling or unable to pay for me to go, but he also thought that, being bilingual, I had a natural career choice as an English teacher. At that time, he worked as the English teacher at a private school, the only basic education school that offered English as a second language.

The requirement for becoming an English teacher in the private or semiprivate sector was a Certificate of Aptitude from the Official Language School in La Coruña. Native speakers had to do a dual exam to prove they had an adequate command of the Spanish language. I had no desire to be a teacher, so this led me to drop out of high school when I was sixteen and take over the running of our small-holding. Originally, we had chickens, rabbits, a pig, a sheep, and a small herd of goats and a very large vegetable garden. This proved to be a blessing, as from the age of fifteen until I left home at eighteen, I became a vegetarian. I was incapable of eating our own home-reared animals.

During the two years I had run the herd of goats, it had increased to 125 animals. It was hard work and I only had Sunday afternoons free. This had made me realise that I didn't want to be a farmer. Too much hard work, too much heartbreak when things went wrong or when you had to sell the kids, and it was impossible to have a holiday. I had therefore decided to take the exams to achieve the Certificate of Aptitude. It consisted in five exams, each one corresponding to a one-year course. You had the possibility of enrolling just for the exams. They were eliminatory, so you took them all but you had to pass each one before they corrected the next one. I had only gone to school in the UK up to the age of seven and here in Spain I had studied French as a second language. So, I studied grammar from a handbook and enrolled in the first four exams.

That year for the first time, you could take the four exams in Lugo, although you still had to go to La Coruña for the final exam, so I enrolled just to take the four. I got between 90 and a 100 percent in all my exams except for the third year, as there was a section on a compulsory reading book, which I hadn't known about and hadn't read. I was very disappointed as the book was *Rebecca* by Daphne du Maurier, and although I would have had difficulty getting hold of an English copy in Monforte, perhaps someone could have sent me one. But in any case, I still got 85 percent, so I was satisfied with my achievement. I couldn't opt to be a teacher in the state system, as you had to take what is known as*oposiciones*, which are state exams, and the first requirement in those days was to be Spanish.

On my return from my holiday in the UK with my boyfriend, I found that the herd of goats was in the process of being sold. Fortunately, I got back in time to vet the person intending to buy them and to go over my animal registry, which actually was like a small family tree for each goat, with them. Each goat had a name rather than a number (in those days it was unnecessary to have ear tags or to register the animals with any official organisation; that only became norm due to European regulations.) the registry included any illnesses, their descendants, who had sired them, and so on. You may not think it was a professional way to run a herd, but for me it worked, and when the butchers came to buy my kids, they treated them with kid gloves, excuse the pun. I had a fierce reputation and on the few occasions I had taken my kids to the livestock market, I had reduced huge burly men to a quivering heap when they had attempted to manhandle them. In fact, on one occasion, one complained to my stepfather that I had attacked him like "a rabid bitch," to which he replied, "well, be more careful next time!" I was sad to see them go, but it was time to move on.

In the evening of the day they were collected I was having a drink in a bar with my mum and my stepfather, when he shoved a newspaper into my hands, saying, "Here you are! There's a job for you." I surmised that he was as anxious for me to be gone as I was to go.

The advert in question was for native teachers for an academy in Lugo city run by a company based in Vigo, a city in the province of Pontevedra. The conditions were excellent for that time, a maximum of eighteen hours a week for 30,000 pesetas, plus they offered accommodation or, if you preferred to live somewhere else, they would pay an additional 5,000 pesetas towards the rent. I phoned the number provided and was granted an interview in Vigo the following week. Getting to Vigo was an ordeal in those days, before all the new infrastructures built thanks to European funds. It was a three-hour train journey, as I didn't have a car or even a driving license. Luckily, my boyfriend's eldest sister lived in Vigo and she agreed to put us up so we travelled the day before the interview. I was a bit worried that I still had my final exam to take to become properly qualified, but my concerns were unfounded as, for them the most important quality, was the fact that I was a native speaker. I got the job and signed my contract then and there, due to start mid-September. I chose not to accept the offer of accommodation and had the extra 5,000 pesetas included in my pay slip. I had a friend who had been the English teacher at the high school in Monforte and was transferring to Lugo that year. She was flat sharing with another teacher who was also from Monforte and they offered me a room for 5,000 pesetas plus a share in the expenses.

* * * *

My first night in the flat was quite bizarre. Carmen, my friend, wasn't there, so I met my other flat mate for the first time. I was drinking a nice cup of tea when she came into the sitting room and offered me brandy. I was a bit taken aback as I imagined brandy to be something you drank at parties or on a night out, not at home on weekday evening! Anyway, we got talking a bit about ourselves when she suddenly blurted out: "What do you think of gay relationships?" To be honest, I had never thought about them specifically, as a relationship is a relationship and as long as it is of mutual consent, and not breaking any laws, it's fine.

We were only just a few years into democracy in Spain and homosexuals had been persecuted under Franco's dictatorship. However, at the time I was unaware of this as of many things because we had never had a television at home, had always listened to the BBC world service, and I had never socialised much as a teenager. I wasn't sure what she was getting at, but I made it very clear that I didn't tolerate any kind of discrimination. I had had to grow up tough as I had suffered ostracism at school for being a non-Catholic during the year my classmates had been preparing for the Holy Communion, and I had been picked on for being the only foreigner when my village school closed down and we were moved into the larger state school in town. I realise that I never made the slightest effort to fit in, and spending a prolonged period in the UK with my mum when I was nine just unsettled me more. I did find out that if you stood up for your rights, though, you could achieve equality when I discovered that, at twelve, the girls had to serve in the dining room at school but the boys didn't. That soon changed! When I explained my point of view to the headmaster that, of course, I would serve when it was my turn as long as the boys were included in the rota, he was lost for words. I imagine he must have contacted my stepfather, who must have stood by me, as not only was I not expelled but the boys were included in the rota. I guess this didn't do much to increase my popularity. In any case, I need not have reacted so aggressively to Sabela's question as it turned out that she just wanted me to know that her girlfriend would be staying over at the flat and she wanted to make sure I was all right with that.

I found it really surprising that she could think that it might be a problem or that it was necessary to test my reaction. I guess I was very naïve in that sense and quite unaware that in the 80s many people still lived a secret life, worrying about what would be said about them. I was conscious that Monforte was an ultraconservative place and that the people who ran the town at that time were the same people who had been doing so for many years. It was very difficult to get a work permit and residency permit at the time we moved there, and it would have been impossible for my stepfather if he hadn't happened to have been accepted into the right circles. An influential neighbour, who was a member of Opus Dei, had taken a liking to us, and he had introduced my stepfather to all the right people. A very different scenario to the freedom of movement for workers under the EU.

Due to the circles my family moved in, I had spent most of my teenage years hiding and sneaking about, as there were many places I was not allowed to go to and things I was not allowed to do and everybody in town, even the feared "*maderos*", as everyone called the police, due to their brown uniforms (which had replaced the grey ones that they had worn during the dictatorship), knew me. I was lucky because I left home and that suffocating environment at eighteen, but many of my peers, mostly the children of these influential people, had a much harder time and a great many of them chose drugs to escape the pressure. So, I shouldn't have been surprised that there were not only restrictions on the places we could go to and the things we could do, but also on who we could go out with.

The following afternoon, I had a meeting with my boss in Lugo. Fortunately, the person I had had the original interview with was also present, as my boss tried to get me to move into the accommodation they provided. However, I had a copy of the advertisement where it clearly stated that if the employees preferred to find alternative lodgings, they were entitled to 5,000 pesetas towards the rent and I said this had been agreed to in Vigo. I also informed them that I had had my contract checked by a lawyer in Monforte and that I was aware they had to process my work permit so I could obtain my residency permit. I briefly met my colleagues, a lovely girl from Ireland who had been recruited there and had just arrived from the airport, and a young lad whose parents were Galician but who had been born in the UK. I was dismissed from the meeting, but a short time after I found out that Kathryn's contract had been changed and that she had to work longer hours than originally agreed and was being paid a lower rate. She didn't speak Spanish and didn't have enough money to go home, so she agreed to the new terms. I was very lucky that I was in a much stronger position, although after working there for eight months, my paperwork was finally rejected, as the authorities didn't consider that it was a specialised job that couldn't be done by Spaniards. By this time, of course, after wanting to return to the UK for the past ten years, I had decided to stay. However, as my paperwork had been rejected, I had to rethink my options. So, I got married to my boyfriend. But that's another story . . .

Where the Wood Nymphs Weep

Liza Grantham

Now autumn's dwindling sunlight swathes the wooded valleys,
The pallid rays seep idly through the dells,
Where oaks, once proud, have lost their robes of emerald,
Their erstwhile majesty barely remembered
In a carpet of russet and gold, where the wood nymphs creep.

Then comes the first chill of winter on the wind,
Stealing softly down the hillside, carrying its whispered warning
The forest, hushed and weary, heeds the call to slumber
And the humbled oaks yield to the spell of Morpheus
Cast through the deepest darkness where the wood nymphs sleep.

The cuckoo's ostinato heralds spring's arrival
And a rousing chorus in crescendo fills the air
The wakening forest rings with vibrant harmony
And the mighty oaks rejoice in the promise of renaissance
Stirring in their budding branches where the wood nymphs peep.

The sun burns fiercely into summer, oppressive and relentless,
Wielding Vulcan's curse: A glint! A spark! A flame!
A merciless inferno rages through the choking woodlands
Where the valiant oaks fall helplessly to their cruel fate,
Their remains charred and smould'riing where the wood nymphs
weep.

About the Authors

Stephen Bush

Born in Singapore and an Australian citizen, now lives in southern Europe. He is the publisher for Cyberworld Publishing, is volume editor for the annual *The Good Life in Galicia* anthology; the author of the novel *My Sister's Funeral*; short story writer; and author of dog care and grooming manuals.

Adrián Casanova Chiclana

Adrián Casanova Chiclana, Galician born, says he enjoys writing because he considers it a natural and silent means of communication among people who are far apart. Writing is a powerful tool, which can stir up intense feelings and emotions. He usually writes in the Galician language because he believes it is a breath of fresh air, reminiscent of the scent of damp earth after the first drops of rain. He has previously taken part in several competitions in this language, obtaining second place in the Xuventude Crea (2016), a short story competition organized by the Xunta de Galicia and being short-listed in the competition O Lugar Onde Vivo, Relatos polo Territorio (2014), organized by ADEGA Publishing and the Diputation of Lugo. He describes himself as an inquisitive person who has many interests and an entropy lover. For this reason, he belongs to a cultural association called Náufragos do Paradiso, which aims to turn the Ribeira Sacra into a cultural paradise besides being a place of natural beauty, of extensive Romanesque heritage and the cradle of the famous Ribeira Sacra wines. #P.S.:Love the Planet.

Vanesa de la Puenta Blanco

I was born in Vitoria Gasteiz in 1980, where I still live

I have two children, Izaro and Julen. They are the principal reason I have every day to get up and live, but not the only one: my husband, my parents, my cousin M and the rest of my family and friends are very important for me, too.

My grandparents will be always in my mind and in my heart. I love them.

I love Galicia. I love literature.

I love going through reality to my dreams.
I love loving.

Liza Grantham

Liza Grantham is from England and has lived in Galicia for seven years. She has written for pleasure since childhood, winning her first poetry competition at the age of eleven. As a primary teacher for over twenty years she enjoyed working with children on performance poetry and drama.

Liza loves the tranquillity of life in her remote *aldea*, where she and her husband make a total of only five residents. In addition to the many labours that come with a rustic lifestyle she spends her free time walking her dog, knitting, sewing, compiling cryptic crosswords and writing poetry, drama and memoirs. She has a passion for cooking and creating her own recipes, always on the look-out for new guinea-pigs to join her dinner table!

Dawn Hawkins

Dawn, hails from Doncaster the home of Michael Parkinson. She attended one of the oldest grammar schools in the UK, founded in 1350

She now lives near Sarria, in Galicia northern Spain. Her home is a typical Galician granite farmhouse, bought as a ruin. She and her partner have spent 10 years creating a habitable space and, although not completed, she now has a space to write and follow her other passion, cooking.

She lives with Steve, the love of her life and husband of 40 years. He has the knack of producing coffee at the salient moment. Especially first thing in the morning

They have three sheep who are professional eaters, organic rabbits, ducks and chickens for the table. Tania, Rowan, and Franki, two rescue dogs and a cat, have the run of the garden, orchard, and field and are her early warning system for visitors.

She also writes under the name of A. D. Thorne.

Andrea Jones Jones

Andrea Jones was born in the UK but grew up in Galicia. She left the UK at the age of seven with her mother and stepfather and, after traveling throughout Europe and other parts of Spain, they settled in a small village close to the town of Monforte de Lemos. Mother of four, she has lived for different periods in Burgos and other parts of Galicia, including a short time in Muxía on the famous Death Coast. Finally having returned to Monforte de Lemos, she currently works as a teacher of both English and Spanish. She enjoys writing in her spare time.

Jennifer Juan

Jennifer Juan is a cultural melting pot of an artist. She is a writer, a musician, a film maker and a podcast host. A tornado of darkness and delicacy, Juan creates engaging and powerful projects, using a variety of mediums and platforms, each dripping with her signature playful, yet powerful style of writing.

Beginning her journey as an artist as a teenager, Juan graduated from The University of Greenwich in 2013, and began sharing her work on her personal website, *JenniferJuan.com*, posting written poetry and video projects, including the immersive poetry podcast, *Sincerely, Jennifer x*, which has amassed over 15,000 listeners since it began in 2017. She has also released several printed volumes of poetry, including the critically acclaimed *"Home Wrecker"*, and in 2018 *"27, With A White Lighter"*.

Sarah Newton-John

Sarah is 53, from New South Wales, in Australia, and has worked in offices in Sydney for 30 years. She is now enjoying a newfound country life away from the hustle and bustle, with the time to write the occasional poem and read the work of other talented contributors. She is blessed to be in green, tranquil Galicia, co-owning a small bed and breakfast, with her lovely partner, and sharing it with their chihuahua, Rafael and cat, Tabby.

Michelle Northwood

Michele travelled the world for twenty years as a professional dancer, magician and fire-eater. When she retired, she went to work in Galicia as a holiday rep. She met her future husband, Randy, in the hotel featured in the story and although the narrative is fictional, the interactions with the tourists did actually take place.

Currently, she lives in a countryside finca in mainland Spain and shares her home with her husband, three dogs, three cats and two terrapins. However, Galicia will always have a special place in her heart and, once a year, she travels back there to visit her in laws.

Michele has a First Class Honours Degree in Modern Languages (English and Spanish) and runs her own Language School where she prepares children and adults for the prestigious Cambridge English examinations.

She has also just published her first book, '*Fishnets In The Far East*' which is an autobiography.

Heath Savage

Heath Savage (58) has lived and worked in the UK, USA, Belgium, and Australia. She graduated from the University of Stirling with a degree in History and English Literature in 1987. She obtained post-graduate qualifications in counselling and case management from the Australian College of Applied Psychology. Heath has pursued three successful career paths: community work, vocational training, and commercial cooking.

Heath now lives and works in Galicia's Ribeira Sacra region, where she and her partner run a boutique B&B in a three-hundred-year-old stone farmhouse.

Heath is a chef, writer, blogger and gardener, currently working on three titles, one of which is a Travel/Recipe book featuring local Galician produce. She currently writes a weekly article in The Local Spain.

J. P. Vincent

J. P. Vincent is the penname of Jacqueline Suffolk. A bubbly British blonde, Jacqueline now lives in Galicia, with her sainted partner, John. They share life with a Galician cat called Freddie who was found living, with his mum, under their roof. They spend their time renovating their old stone house, rebuilding barns, and also 200 meters of dry stone walling, which to date they've completed about a tenth of. They also have half a mountain to do something with when they run out of other things to do.

Jacqueline loves to travel. She and John spent many years touring Europe in their motorhome, La Gorda, and she loves to write about travelling. Her bus route No.83 article is in the latest edition of the Bradt Travel Guide "Bus Pass Britain." She is also a consultant for Motorhome Monthly Magazine (MMM) where her remit is to answer queries regarding motorhome travel in northern Spain and Portugal.

Lisa R. Wright

Lisa and partner Stewart moved to Galicia in 2007 giving up promising careers messing about in ponds as ecologists to renovate a semi-derelict stone house, grow veggies to eat (when the mice don't get there first), and to raise chickens and rabbits.

In 2010 they married in Galicia. An event which delighted locals, who got to pelt them with rice, and the local council who gave them a nice ceramic plaque bearing the *Concello* coat of arms to commemorate the occasion.

In 2014, having *almost* finished renovating their house, they bought another in the same *aldea*. This time for Lisa's mum, Iris, who has lived in Galicia very happily since 2015.

None of them can imagine living anywhere else.

~

Previous
The Good life in Galicia
Anthologies

The Good Life in Galicia 2018

The third collection in the series.

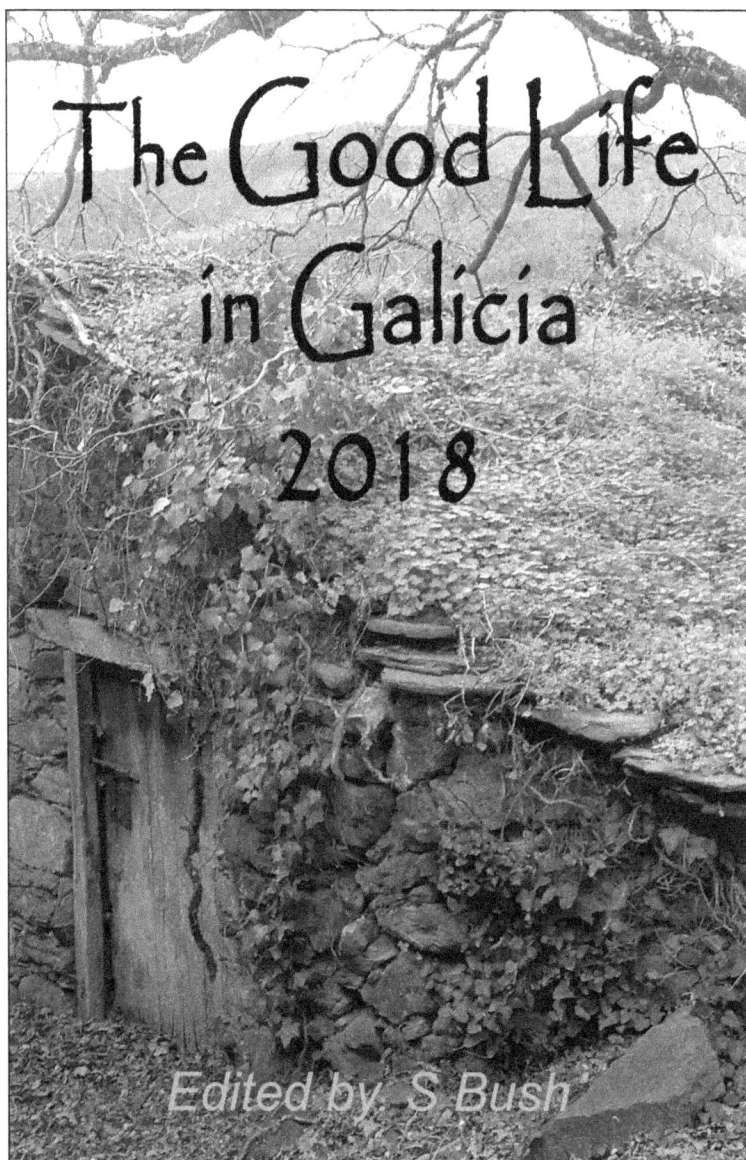

The Good life in Galicia 2017

The second collection in the series.

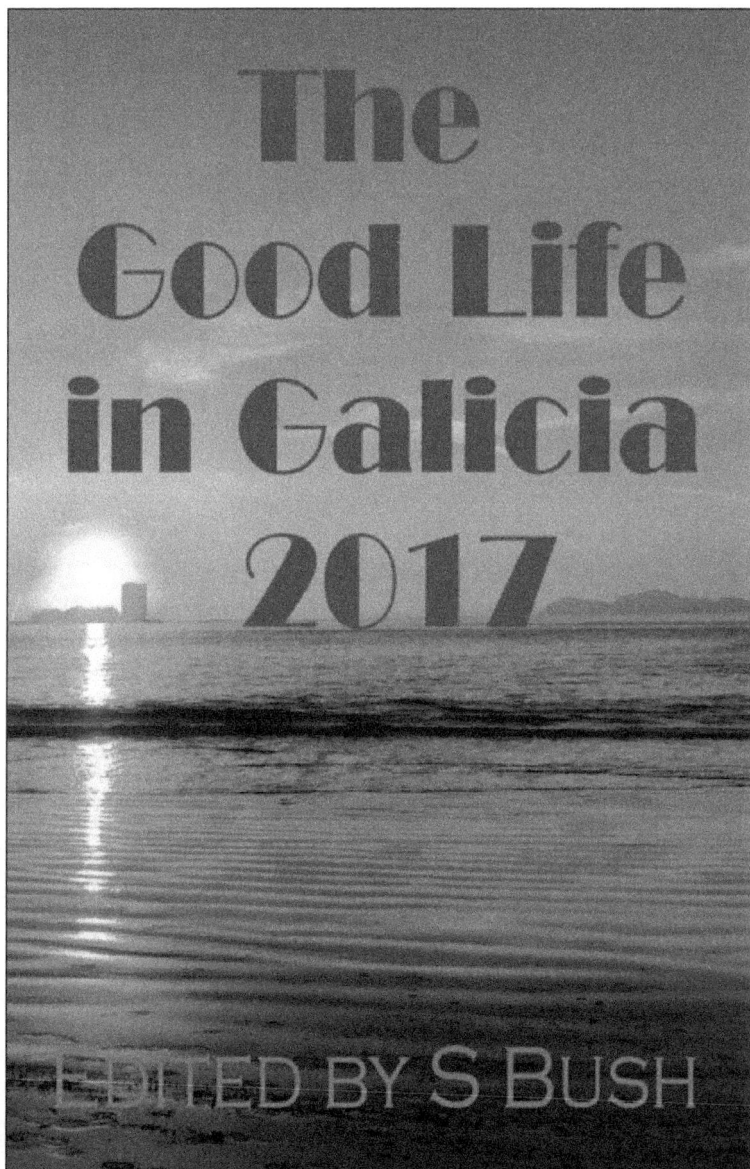

The Good Life in Galicia 2017

EDITED BY S BUSH

The Good life in Galicia 2016

The first collection in the series.

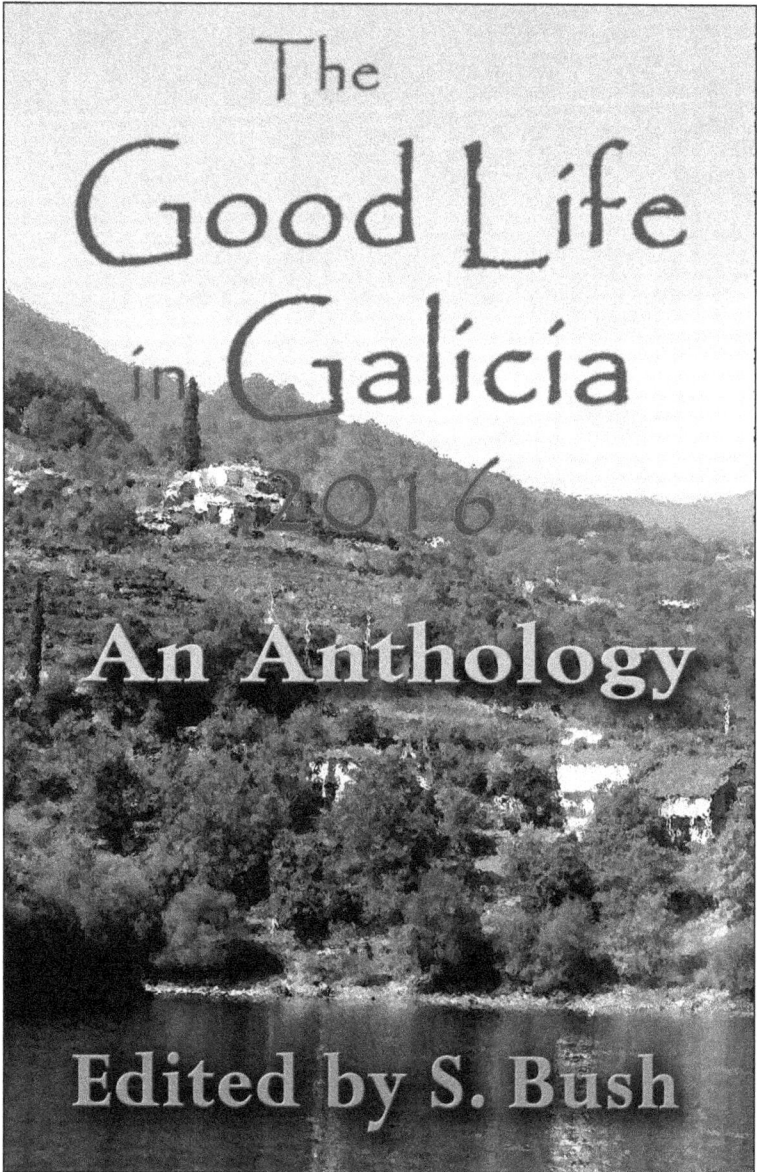

Cyberworld Publishing

"The Good Life in Galicia" 2020 Competition

Short story competition and anthology

In 2016 Cyberworld Publishing produced The Good Life in Galicia 2016 after running a competition for short prose pieces in the categories of fiction and nonfiction.
In 2017 we added a poetry category and in 2019 we are again seeking prose pieces in the categories of fiction and nonfiction, and poetry.

Submissions/Entries:

Prose: Fiction and non fiction 1,200 to 4,500 words in ENGLISH
Poetry: max 45 lines in ENGLISH
Prizes: 15 Euros first place and 5 Euros second place in each section, prose fiction, prose non fiction and poetry (paid via Paypal).
All entries must be available to be published in the anthology "The Good Life in Galicia 2019" in e-book and paperback.
Entries to be published will be selected by the volume editors and not all entries may be included (No payments will be made for publication.).

Entries:

- Closing date is 1 August 2020

- All works must be about Galicia in a significant way.

- No requirement for the author/s to have ever been to Galicia

- All entries are to be sent by e-mail to thegoodlifeingalicia2017 ATT outlook dot com

- Entries to be pasted into the e-mail, not sent as attachments.

- All Entries to be in English.

- Files to be in .rtf or .doc 2003 format NO .docx. Font: 12 point Arial. Style: Normal. No Headings style please.

- Direct all enquiries to thegoodlifeingalicia2017 ATT outlook dot com

- You can find more information and updates for the competition at: www.CyberworldPublishing.com
And on Facebook at Cyberworld Publishing

DEADLINE: First of August 2020

www.ingramcontent.com/pod-product-compliance
Lightning Source LLC
Chambersburg PA
CBHW031559040426
42452CB00006B/350